LAND YOUR DREAM JOB. KILL IT IN
YOUR CAREER. ROCK SOCIAL MEDIA.

ALIZA LICHT

Foreword by Donna Karan

piatkus

PIATKUS

First published in the US in 2015 by Grand Central Publishing,
a division of Hachette Book Group, Inc.
First published in Great Britain in 2015 by Piatkus

1 3 5 7 9 10 8 6 4 2

Copyright © Aliza Licht 2015

A CIP catalogue record for this book
is available from the British Library.

ISBN 978-0-349-40854-5

Printed and bound in Great Britain by
Clays Ltd, St Ives plc

Papers used by Piatkus are from well-managed forests
and other responsible sources.

MIX
Paper from
responsible sources
FSC
www.fsc.org   FSC® C104740

To David, Jonathan and Sabrina,
I love you more than the world.

In loving memory of my father,
Dr. Michael Bernfeld, who left his mark
on everyone who knew him.

TABLE OF INSPIRATION

FOREWORD BY DONNA KARAN

People with passion inspire me. You feel their energy. They stir your deepest emotions. They create momentum and excitement. We can't help but be drawn in and want to be around them. When it comes to your career, you can't hope to succeed unless you have passion for what you do. Passion is everything.

Aliza Licht has a true passion for fashion. For the seventeen years she's worked at Donna Karan International, I've seen it firsthand. Aliza expresses her passion in what I call my "C" words—she connects, communicates and collaborates. She does it with clothes, creativity, celebrities, conversation, community. (Half a million Twitter followers is some community!) So naturally, she has chosen to write a book about yet another "C" word: careers. I can't think of a better mentor to help get you going at work and in life.

I'm passionate about mentoring because I owe so much to those who have mentored me over the years. My most influential mentor was Anne Klein, my first boss. She taught me to trust my instincts. Anne also had an amazing work ethic, which is why she fired me when she thought I wasn't taking my job seriously. I was nineteen and devastated. Soon after, I got a job with Patti Cappalli, another designer who became a mentor. I worked incredibly hard and learned the importance of discipline. A year later, Anne Klein was looking for an assistant designer, and I applied. Thankfully, Anne gave me a second chance. When Anne suddenly passed away a few years later, I was asked to take over the label. And the rest, as they say, is history.

Anne and Patti were remarkably generous with me. In different ways, they showed me designing was a business, one you have to work at. As a result of their example, mentoring young talent is one of my greatest pleasures. Whenever possible, I work with design students at Parsons The New School for Design, happy to give back in any way I can.

Mentors shape who we are. They guide us and let us learn from their successes and their failures. They're the ultimate big sister in our professional lives. They give you room to grow and help you realize who you are and what you're capable of doing. They give you that needed nudge, that sign of encouragement. They challenge you to be your best, and if they're good, they're also tough on you. Because mentors aren't there to flatter you; they're there to help you.

Everyone may not be as lucky as I was to find a great mentor, which is where this book comes in. Aliza is the ultimate mentor because she's the ultimate role model. She talks the talk and walks the walk. A self-starter, Aliza makes things happen. Everything is possible with Aliza, and if she doesn't know something, she's the first to reach out and find someone who does. Like all great communicators, Aliza is about the "we," not the "me."

Most importantly, Aliza is open to new ideas and new ways of doing things. She was on top of social media long before the rest of us. The success of DKNY PR GIRL is testimony to the force of her personality. She gives you a reason to keep checking in for brand news, insider gossip and girl-talk. Aliza saw social media for the incredible platform it can be.

Aliza's Internet success reminds me of when I started my company. My goal was to design clothes for just me and my friends. Little did I know I had so many friends! Yet that's what success is all about—believing in something and going for it. If it speaks to you, the chances are great that it speaks to a lot of other people, too.

Aliza knows communication is all about the personal touch. She's conversational, she's witty, she shares. She is connected to the world, because she first connects on a personal level. She can't help it; it's in her DNA. As Aliza puts it, this book isn't a "how-to," it's a "must do"! Read it, be inspired—then go out and own your passion.

A NOTE ON THE PEOPLE AND PLACES IN
LEAVE YOUR MARK

The stories in this book are authentic accounts of experiences I have had or been privy to throughout my career, told to the best of my recollection. For the most part, I have changed the names, gender or character traits of some of the people mentioned in this book. To that end, I have also changed some stories' chronology or setting.

The titles of the fashion magazines I worked at in the past have also been changed to chic, French titles. I could have totally included the real publication names, but what's the fun in that? You should also know that the circumstances and working conditions that I describe at these magazines occurred many, many years ago and may not be a reflection of what happens today.

For the purpose of flow, I made a decision to pick a lane between sexes. Meaning, no matter the story, I have chosen between using the pronouns "he," "she," "her" and "him" at random. Feel free to recast the person as you see fit.

The advice and insider secrets provided in this book are strictly and exclusively my view. They are lessons I have learned along the way and do not reflect the views of my employers past or present.

INTRODUCTION

"Who wore it better?" flashed across my computer screen. As a public relations executive working for one of the most internationally renowned luxury fashion brands, following style trends, celebrity red carpet coverage and the like, is a daily part of my job. Was Charlize's lace Dior dress styled as well as Cate's Armani? What fashion contraption was Gaga wearing now? I loved contemplating things like that, but this time was different.

I had stumbled upon a random post from a fashion blog cleverly comparing the dress worn by my company's Twitter avatar—a hand-drawn "fashion girl" illustration—to none other than Jennifer Lopez, who happened to be wearing an identical blush draped jersey Donna Karan dress. Was this blogger *really* comparing an illustrated fashion persona to a real A-list celebrity? *Nicely done*, I thought. Whether this blogger intended to get my attention or not, she had succeeded in grabbing it.

Upon quickly scrolling through the site, I learned that the blogger's name was Jenna and that she lived in Austin, Texas. She was clearly good at dissecting style, and her writing was sarcastic, a personality trait that I happen to love in people. I decided to follow her on Twitter.

As weeks passed, we became Twitter-friendly, tweeting

back and forth every once in a while to dish about this or that. One day, I received a direct message from her asking me if she could email me a few career-related questions. Jenna's request was one that I had received countless times before—especially on Twitter. And since mentoring has always been a passion of mine, I immediately responded with my email address.

Within minutes, I received an email from Jenna. Actually, it wasn't an email; it was a novel. Jenna told me that she worked at an artificial turf–manufacturing company, but that she loved fashion and really wanted to break into the field. It continued for paragraphs. I knew that the answers she needed were vast. I responded by simply writing, "CALL ME."

A few minutes later my phone rang. Jenna and I spoke for a really long time and it was almost as if we were good friends catching up. (There's just something about the sense of community you feel with people you meet through Twitter.) I had a lot of advice to give and the bottom line was that if she wanted to break into fashion, she needed to be in New York. *Sigh*. I know that's so much easier said than done. It's hard to just pick up, leave your friends and family and move to another state with no job to speak of. In fact, it's frightening, not to mention *really* expensive. I knew that Jenna must have hung up the phone with a heavy heart and a swirling head.

One afternoon about five months later, while I was online catching up on Paris Fashion Week, I saw a tweet from Jenna asking people to vote for her in a blogger competition. The prize was a yearlong blogging position in New York. Along with some of her other Twitter friends, I retweeted her request, encouraging people to vote. She ended up becoming a finalist and was flown to New York. We made a plan to meet. When Jenna came to the office, it was like seeing an old friend that I hadn't seen in years.

A month later, Jenna learned that she had unfortunately lost the blogger competition, but she wasn't about to give up. Through her online network, she discovered that there was a social media position available at a public relations agency in New York. Her previous trip to New York, along with this opportunity, had solidified what she had been feeling since our initial phone conversation: She had to move here.

Without another thought, Jenna proceeded to pack up her life in Austin and move to New York City. With no apartment and no job, she would stay on a friend's couch and get a job checking coats to make some money. When Jenna called and told me what she'd done, I couldn't help but be impressed. She had taken our conversation very seriously. She was hungry. She wanted a career in fashion and she was going to do anything to get it. *Good for her.*

Sometimes when you take a chance, you get lucky. A week after Jenna moved to New York, she secured an interview at that PR agency. Before the interview, Jenna politely asked me if I would consider being a reference for her. To be clear, I don't give out references lightly. I had never actually worked with Jenna, but I felt like I knew her social media skills from her blog and her tweets, and I knew that I liked her as a person. Sure, that's not rock-solid evidence that she should get the reference, but I always go with my gut, and my gut said that she would be an asset to any company that hired her. Jenna nailed the interview and a week later was offered the job.

Six months after that, I was faced with hiring a new

assistant, and I wanted to find someone who also had social media experience. I decided that the best way to find the most socially savvy candidates was online. So I tweeted a link inviting candidates to apply on my company's Facebook page, stating publicly why they thought they should get the job. After that, they were instructed to also send their cover letter and resumé to human resources. When my job-posting tweet popped up on Jenna's timeline, she knew she had to move quickly. As it turned out, and unbeknownst to me at the time, Jenna had just been laid off.

By this point, Jenna and I were very friendly, so she might have thought to casually email me and write, "Hey, I want this job! Oh and P.S., I just got laid off." That statement would have totally been in line with her colorful personality. Except she didn't. She behaved professionally and applied properly, a move that I greatly appreciated.

We received over three hundred applications for the assistant position. You would be amazed by how many of those people completely blew it on the very first step of the application process. The typos were staggering. The text-message speak was even worse. People treated the application process quite like they behave socially—very, very casually. But they shouldn't have, because it was a test. I wanted to see if the people applying were savvy enough to know how to switch gears between social talk and professional communication. Most didn't. My mind couldn't help but go back to Jenna and how she intuitively knew the difference. But could it be that easy? Did I already find the perfect person for the job on Twitter a year earlier? I couldn't fathom it, so I labored over hundreds of submissions anyway and ultimately met with ten people. In the end, after a long, drawn-out process, Jenna was the one. One tweet from a girl who worked at an artificial turf–manufacturing company in Austin led to her dream job in fashion, in the heart of New York City.

———

Jenna's story is the ultimate example of everything I believe in and everything I will teach you in this book. We live in a world that is totally and utterly connected. If managed properly, how you make and use those connections can result in amazing things. Jenna's clear talent and instinct to behave in the professional way she did made me want to help her. But she's not the only one.

Since 2009, I have had the daily privilege of sharing my fashion insider views on the glamorous, and sometimes *not-so-glamorous*, world of fashion in one hundred and forty characters or less on Twitter. Since that time, I have organically built a loyal community of over half a million followers—or as I like to call them, "Twitter friends." Whether I'm tweeting about Oscar gowns that have gone missing at LAX or the ridiculous fashion show ticket requests that come into my inbox, my tweets offer a juicy behind-the-scenes peek at fashion through the lens of public relations. But something interesting happened on this six-year journey: Social media has become just as much a vehicle for me to mentor as it is to dish on the insides of the fashion world.

Thousands of conversations have shown me that no matter the industry, everyone is just trying to make it. People need others to lift them up when they are down or steer them in another direction when they are headed the wrong way. I speak to people who need a complete motivation makeover and others who just don't know where to begin. These conversations have led to many a coffee, meeting with people who want to brainstorm about how to make their next career move. I get it. I would have *loved* to go for coffee with someone who had already made some of the hard decisions I was trying to make back in the day. While I've always been one to pay it forward, how can you have coffee with everyone who asks? You simply can't.

Leave Your Mark is my way of allowing us to grab that coffee. In this book I will spill all the secrets I've learned the hard way and help you land your dream job, *kill it* in your career, rock social media and build your personal brand.

———

Forget everything you have ever learned. My experience in the fashion industry, and specifically in public relations, is the only crash course you will ever need. Hint: We're not playing here, *so get ready.* I will share with you insider tips to help you navigate your career in *any* industry. I will teach you all the ways I have learned to get ahead that no one ever tells you. Things like: what you're supposed to do when you've made the wrong career choice and figure it out way too late, or how to get experience when you have none. I will show you how to suck your internship dry and interview strategically for the job of your dreams. I will teach you how to assess if you're ready for that promotion and how to negotiate it with flair. You will learn how to survive office politics and all the things you should *never* say to your boss. When you realize that you're at a dead-end job, I will show you how to shift gears. I will demonstrate how social media can benefit (or damage) your reputation and how to make presentations like a pro. And when you've finally made it up the corporate ladder, I will share with you the merits of being a likeable, motivating leader.

But probably the most important thing that I will impart to you is that YOU are your own brand, and how you manage your personal brand can make or break your career.

Because here's the biggest secret truth: How you brand and market yourself can weigh just as heavily on your success as your actual skills do. As a publicist, it's my job to shape messaging and generate publicity. When you spend all day strategizing how to make people perceive a brand positively like I do, you start to realize that the same principles can be applied to people. ***How you communicate and influence others often matters more than the idea you're pitching.*** I will show you how to create and shape your own personal brand by manipulating the principles of public relations from both the fashion and celebrity worlds as a guide.

My career in public relations led to my expertise in social media. Not only has social media turned "traditional public relations" on its head, it has also shown us how influence matters and how it can grow from anywhere. I will explain in detail how to use social media in creating your personal brand. You will see how real engagement and transparency matter and how connecting with people can help shape and build your image.

My knowledge comes from nearly twenty years of experience, but isn't it a shame that we often don't get to have that experience until it's *too late*? Sure, we all have to make mistakes, but wouldn't it be genius if we didn't have to make as many? I want to give you a cheat sheet: everything I've learned. I want you to have choices and to be savvy enough to recognize the options in front of you. But more than that, I want you to see that you have the power to create a new path for yourself where there isn't one. **Why wait to learn something the hard way when I can teach you now?**

Leave Your Mark isn't a "how-to" book; it is a "must-do" book...OK, and definitely a lot of "don't-dos." In this book I'll take you along my career journey—which, I promise you, was anything but a smooth ride. You will see the good, the bad, the ugly, the insane and the hilarious. Since making the hard decision to give up medicine to pursue my childhood love of fashion, I have pretty much seen and heard it all. At every step of my career, I have learned incredible lessons that you can use *no matter what job you have*. The lessons in this book will also prove valuable to anyone who simply wants to be a better communicator, conveying their personal brand in a more impactful way.

Life is too short to settle. You have the power to create your own path to success. But I will warn you, this journey doesn't come without a lot of soul-searching and, ultimately, hard work. Nothing is yours unless you work for it—and however hard you think you have to work in order to get somewhere, I can promise you that it's triple.

I know that sometimes life can be daunting and that obstacles can seem insurmountable, but with this book, a massive to-do list and a giant cup of coffee, I promise that you can get it all done and still have time to tweet about it.

PART I

Landing Your Dream Job

CHAPTER ONE

Finding the Right Career Path

GROWING UP, MOST OTHER TEENAGERS I KNEW WERE WALLPAPERING THEIR ROOMS WITH PICTURES OF THEN-HEARTTHROBS COREY HAIM AND Jason Patric. But not me. My walls were plastered with high-fashion magazine spreads. It was 1988 and *Vogue* had just gotten a new editor in chief, a British import named Anna Wintour who had new ideas for the magazine. *Vogue's* covers, for example, had featured tightly cropped photos for years. Anna's first cover featured a half-body shot of Israeli model Michaela Bercu dressed in a Christian Lacroix haute couture top paired with—drumroll, please—Guess jeans.

That cover was groundbreaking—not only for the way Anna let the reader see more of the model, but for how couture was paired with off-the-rack clothing. It was just unheard of at the time. The genius behind that breakthrough marriage of high-low styling was Carlyne Cerf de Dudzeele, a French fashion editor whose love for color, accessories and eccentric styling made for a very creative and inspiring bedroom wall. That cover was the focal point of my bedroom door for months.

For me, fashion was what life should be like, just amplified. A world worth diving into and living in, albeit through images. I spent years sitting on my bed, doing homework and glancing up at those fashion-plastered walls. But the joke was that I never once gave even a single thought as to how a magazine was created. As far as I was concerned, all of those issues made their way to the newsstand and onto my walls like magic. Fashion wasn't a career option—if only because I didn't know any better and had no one to guide me.

Because I had always liked and done well in science and my father was a reputable dentist with his own practice, I decided to study to become a doctor. I was good with my hands, so my love of art sparked a more specific interest in plastic surgery—a specialty that, in my mind, combined the best of both worlds, beauty and science.

During high school I began interning for a nearby plastic surgeon whose office was straight out of the movie *Pleasantville*. A white picket fence surrounded his perfect little white-shingled house, where procedures happened all day long, rarely with any drama. I had a front-row seat in the operating room, watching cosmetic surgeries that all looked so seamless. I loved that a plastic surgeon was in the business of making people feel better about themselves, not to mention how fun it was to see your friend's mom getting a face-lift when she doesn't know you're standing there watching. *Haha.* I was certain that plastic surgery was the right path for me. That experience, plus my grades, earned me a full four-year merit scholarship to the University of Maryland, where I'd been awarded the title "Francis Scott Key scholar." My parents were over the moon: Their daughter was premed—and for free! They couldn't sign the paperwork fast enough.

I declared my major in neurobiology and physiology and sucked up eight a.m. labs four days a week, eating candy corn to keep me awake. (I didn't drink coffee...yet.) I took the dreaded MCATs during my junior year and landed a six-week summer internship at a hospital in Long Island. I was so excited that I'd been accepted into the program and confident that the experience would prove valuable and educational.

That summer, my alarm went off every day at six a.m. Getting ready was easy because it didn't really matter what I wore. I'd be covering it all up with a lab coat   unless I was doing surgical rounds, which meant changing into scrubs, a hairnet and a face mask. Every day at seven thirty a.m., the interns were briefed on that day's schedule. Our program was meant to show us what it was really like being a doctor.

Each morning exposed us to difficult cases, so by the time lunch came around, we couldn't wait to sit down together in the cafeteria to relax and reflect on our experiences that morning. Everyone had strong opinions about whatever medical course of action was taken or needed. Listening to everyone's point of view, I slowly began to realize that I didn't share the passion or enthusiasm they did for what we were doing. But how could that be? I loved everything I was learning in school and during my plastic surgery internship, but hated the practical applications of those lessons in a hospital? It didn't make sense. But an uncomfortable feeling started to nag at me, and with every day that passed, it became more difficult to ignore.

I would spend all day in the hospital and then come home to my ailing grandma who lived with us after having had a stroke thirteen years earlier. It was wonderful to live with her—she was a remarkable person—but it was also extremely sad to watch her deteriorate. My time at the hospital and my home life combined were physically and emotionally draining.

On Friday afternoons when I came home from the hospital, I couldn't wait to shower and pick out my outfit for the night. Fashion excited me and on top of everything else, I hated that it didn't matter what I wore each day. I missed my clothes. It was like someone had snipped my wings. Wearing scrubs was awful; they made me feel very self-conscious and just plain dumpy. The hairnets we had to wear during surgical rounds were mortifying (imagine wearing a shower cap out in public) and the face masks smudged my signature red lipstick. Medical wardrobe is clearly not a reason to give up on a profession, but I was looking for any excuse I could find to convince myself that the career path I was on was the wrong one. I told myself that if I became a doctor, I would not only be reliving my grandma's long struggle, but I would also be giving up all the fashionable dreams of my youth.

That gut feeling, the one that pulls at you to get your attention, is definitely worth the time to examine. I had to ask myself: Were these reasons big enough to quit medicine? I'd just spent three years working toward a career that I felt like I no longer wanted. But the thought of shifting gears so drastically seemed insane—and shifting them to what? Could I really walk away from a goal I'd had for such a long time? And what would I tell my proud parents?

I had a choice. I could keep calm and carry on despite my reservations, or I could listen to my gut and see what else was out there. I decided that I couldn't live my life with regret. My dream had changed and it wasn't my fault. That's precisely why you intern: to test the water. I had to be honest with myself and admit that it was OK to make a mistake. It's by no means ideal, but it had to be OK. Sticking with medicine would have been the easy path, actually. No explanations necessary, no feeling embarrassed about my mistake. But when everything in your mind is screaming NO, you can't ignore it and you shouldn't ignore it. I had to make a new choice. I had to choose to shut the door on medicine.

I knew there was no easy way to break the news to my parents; we just needed to sit down and have a serious heart-to-heart. So I waited until Saturday morning when it was quiet and I knew I would have their full attention. I wasn't going to sugarcoat it, so I just went straight to the point. "I've been thinking a lot about my experience this summer, and I don't think being a doctor is for me," I said.

Silence.

"What do you mean?" my mom asked cautiously.

"I mean that I am really not happy and I don't think it's because of this one hospital experience," I said. "I don't think I want to be a doctor anymore."

More silence. Maybe shock. I mean, how could they not be disappointed? How many people did they proudly tell that their daughter was going to be a plastic surgeon? I'm sure too many to count.

"So, what do you guys think? Please say something," I said quietly.

"What should we say, Aliza?" (What is worse than when your parents use your actual name?!) "It's your life and your decision. You need to do whatever you think is right for you," my father said.

"But what are you going to do?" pressed my mother.

"I don't know yet," I said nervously. "But I hope to figure it out soon."

With that comment I got up and left the room. My head was swirling. I had spilled the beans but I didn't feel any better. I was very anxious about my mother's last question and also the way she asked it. Her tone was very "You have a plan B, right? Please tell me you have a plan B." Her concern was legitimate. After all, I had only a year of college left. It was too late to change majors. It was too late to do much of anything. Oh and P.S., I had no idea what it actually was that I wanted to do. I needed a really good idea, and you know whenever you need one is precisely when your mind goes blank.

Weeks later, when I was back at school sitting on my bed in my apartment, I glanced at my windowsill, where a copy of *Arthur Elgort's Models Manual* was lying. I had bought that book in my senior year of high school. Elgort, a fashion photographer, filled the pages with stunning images of supermodels, Christy Turlington, Naomi Campbell and Linda Evangelista among them. Completely unreachable, awe-inspiring beauty. Models that Carlyne Cerf de Dudzeele had transformed into supermodels in the 1990s. I had flipped through that book countless times before. But something was different now. Something felt more important.

I suddenly flashed back to my magazine-wallpapered room and it all became crystal clear. Those magazine pages had always been there, right under my nose: Fashion was the answer.

I had spent years gathering magazine editorials to wallpaper my room. It defined who I was. But if you had asked me back then if I wanted to work at a fashion magazine, I would have looked at you like you had five heads. I knew no one working at any magazines or fashion houses. And keep in mind, at that time if you wanted a job, you had to mail your resumé, on paper, into a black hole and wait. I had no networks to draw from: no online job searches, no LinkedIn, not even Google! But at that moment I learned a very important lesson that I have carried throughout my career: You can't just wait for someone to hand you the "in." You have to make it yourself. **INSIDER TIP: If you have no one to show you the ropes, you have to build a ladder.**

Take a Selfie: How Do You Know If You're on the Right Path?

Breaking news: Selfies are not just proof that you wore a great outfit! They can be used for reflection. You need to consider whether you're even in the right hemisphere—geographically and/or metaphorically—for what you want to do. Who says you can't have an "I'm going to be a...*just kidding*!" moment like I did? So what that I spent four years of college prepping for med school? Looking back at all the early warning signs, making the jump to fashion was a natural choice for me.

Bottom line: It's never too late to start over. We hear stories all the time of people later in life going back to school for something completely new and different. Those stories are inspiring. If you're lucky and you're honest with yourself, you might realize that you need to make a change early on.

P.S. this is not a scientific quiz! These are simply questions to ask yourself in order to see your reflection better. Do you honestly know how you really feel about your career choice? Are you afraid of what people will say if you make an about-face? Remind me again whose life it is and how many of them you get? *Yeah, that's what I thought.*

I'm asking you these questions because it's hard to ask these questions of yourself. So, go ahead and check your temperature:

1. How do you feel when you think about embarking on your chosen career path?
   a. happy
   b. excited
   c. indifferent
   d. apprehensive

2. Do you feel passionate about your industry of choice?
   a. yes
   b. not really
   c. not sure
   d. no

3. Are you ready/excited to do the hard work it takes to succeed?
   a. yes
   b. I have no choice
   c. not sure
   d. no

4. Are you envious of another person's career path and wish that you could do something else?
   a. yes
   b. no
   c. sometimes

5. Does your mind ever drift off where you fantasize about doing something else?
   a. all the time
   b. never
   c. sometimes

6. What do you picture yourself doing if you weren't going to stay on your current career path?
   1st choice:
   2nd choice:
   3rd choice:

7. If you could do so without consequences, would you shift gears and choose another path?
   a. yes
   b. no
   c. not sure

8. Are you worried about what others will think if you changed gears?
   a. yes
   b. no
   c. not sure

If the majority of your answers paint the picture of a dissatisfied, non-enthusiastic person, it's time that you seriously rethink your path. It doesn't matter if you're just starting out or are already years down the road. You get one life, but many chances. It's time to take a new one. I'm going to show you how.

We're asked to make decisions that will affect us forever so early in life, and we often feel pressure to stick with the decisions we've made. But let's face it, it's not easy to find a career path. That's why the selfie is important. Self-examination is key. If you're happy with your answers, great. But if you're not, you owe it to yourself to do something about it.

CHAPTER TWO

Getting Experience When You Have No Experience

THE GOOD NEWS WAS, I WAS NOW CLEAR ON WHAT I WANTED: I WANTED TO WORK AT A FASHION MAGAZINE. THE BAD NEWS WAS THAT I HAD JUST spent three years studying neurobiology and physiology, and I was pretty sure my knowledge of organic chemistry was not going to get me very far in fashion. I needed related experience, something to at least move my resumé in the right direction.

The million-dollar question we've all asked ourselves at some point is: How do you get experience when you have no experience?

I decided that the only resource I had was the actual newsstand. Magazines always have a masthead—a page listing everyone on its staff—and I figured it could provide a wealth of information. So I snatched up *DC Moment*, the one regional magazine that looked promising, because its offices were located near my university. If I could somehow land an internship there, I'd be on my way to building that first rung of the ladder. I sent my resumé directly to every senior person on the masthead—*not* only to the human resources department (which, by the way, needs a new name). I figured sending my resumé to human resources would have been like waiting to hear a pin drop in Times Square. I had a gut feeling that I needed to connect with the person who had the job I was trying to get one day. **INSIDER TIP: "To Whom It May Concern" never concerns anyone.**

My resumé was pretty nonexistent, so I had to make my cover letter magical. I knew it would be important to prove to *DC Moment* that I was a fan, so I rounded up the last few issues of the magazine in order to get knowledgeable. Poring over the magazine's content, I made sure to tailor each letter to that editor's specific role at the magazine. **INSIDER TIP: One size cover letter does not fit all.** I wasn't about to tell the restaurant critic how much I loved *DC Moment*'s movie reviews. That may sound obvious, but I can promise you, based on the crap I see, it's not obvious to everybody.

For the next two weeks I checked the mail and my answering machine (that's today's voicemail!) incessantly. One afternoon I came home from class to find a message from an advertising sales representative at *DC Moment* magazine! Either they didn't get a lot of requests for interns or I got lucky. I immediately returned the call.

I didn't want an internship in ad sales *at all*, but I wasn't about to be picky. I needed to get experience and maybe if I proved myself, they would let me moonlight in another department. I had to start somewhere, right? John, the ad sales rep, asked if I could begin immediately and naturally I said yes! Of course I would have to work around my class schedule, but they were amenable to whatever hours I could commit.

Commuting into Washington, DC, three days a week was not an easy task, but I did enjoy getting dressed to go to a real office. The atmosphere there was buzzing with people going to and from. It was an open, newsroom-type floor plan, with lots of desks situated in rows across an open space. People were lively and talkative, which would have made it easy for me to engage. But even though the environment was seemingly relaxed, I felt that I needed to be professional, and in my mind, that meant being serious. I definitely did not want to appear *too* comfortable *too* quickly, because I feared I would somehow suffer for it.

This is one of those weird things—sometimes I think bosses don't like it when you feel at home right off the bat. They want you to struggle a little bit, be a little intimidated and even revere them at the start. I thought then, and still think now, that it's a good idea to let *them* warm up to you instead of the other way around. In general, when people start asking you for your opinion or ask you join them for a meeting, a lunch, whatever…that's proof that you have earned your first stripe. **INSIDER TIP: You're not part of the club until someone tells you that you're part of the club.**

I spent my days at *DC Moment* cold-calling companies to pitch them on buying advertising space in the magazine, a task I found uncomfortable and didn't relish. But I was never going to show John my supervisor that. In fact, I went the opposite route. I powered through my call list so that I could be done as soon as possible. Then I used the extra time to research ads that were being placed in a competitor magazine and *not DC Moment.* I presented those companies to John as possible leads for new business. I wanted to show him that I had drive and that I was creative. He was impressed.

Once I knew there was nothing more I could do for the ad sales team on any given workday, I would wander around the office to see what everyone else was up to. I needed to get experience beyond just making cold calls, because in the back of my mind, I knew I had to work on honing actual skills. As I'd originally suspected, I loved hanging with the people over in editorial, those who got to write about restaurant openings and cool new gadgets they liked. Even though I was technically an ad sales intern, I offered to help them any way I could once my own work for the day was done. **INSIDER TIP: When you're done with your to do list, make your own work or ask for more.**

I wanted to absorb as much as I could and make myself available to every possible opportunity so that I'd have more comprehensive content to include on my resumé. By being so amenable to every task, I also made a lot of friends. I turned into the office's intern, one who knew and was willing to help everyone. But making lemonade out of lemons wasn't enough; I wanted to learn where I could get the lemons in the first place. That's what I did at *DC Moment*; I learned all the parts of the business and how every area of the magazine came together to make the whole. I asked a lot of questions about the bigger picture and I got a lot of answers. When I was done I knew much more than when I had started.

Throughout my later career, I've encountered way too many interns who *don't* do that. Most interns don't take advantage of the wealth of information before them and it's a real shame. You can't just float by in an internship. You can't be what I call a "zombie intern." You know the type—she's there, she does everything asked of her, but there's no pulse, no passion, no real understanding of the bigger picture. When a zombie's internship comes to an end, she always asks for a reference and I'm always like, "Really? Do I even know you?" She ultimately learns the hard way. **INSIDER TIP: Use your internship to start thinking and acting like you're already a professional.**

A good resumé should make you appear at least a year ahead of your age or assumed experience level. I always love when I see recent graduates who have four years of internship experience. It shows me that they have not wasted a minute and that they know how important it is to take advantage of the opportunities out there. Too many students think college is a vacation, but the smart ones know they can't just waste that time playing.

Relevant experience on a resumé is always impressive, but sometimes seems impossible. You need to take what you can get and mold any experience to work for you. No matter the industry, you need to find those professional common denominators. **INSIDER TIP: As long as the experience is related (and I mean loosely related) to your passion in some way, it's worth your time and effort.** Also, by taking an internship or job that's not on your firmly designated career path, you may learn something new about yourself.

Advertising sales was never going to be right for me. I knew that intuitively before I ever stepped foot in *DC Moment*. But instead of counting it out, I welcomed it in a different way. I saw that internship as an opportunity to test my skills in an environment that I secretly didn't really *care* about. It's like dating. "I like you as a friend" are brutally honest words that nobody wants to hear. But the funny thing about hearing them is that it takes the pressure completely off. Since he's not going to like you in *that* way anyway, you may as well just be yourself. The same thing applies when you're interning in a field that you don't ultimately want to work in. You're not afraid to be yourself and you're not as intimidated, so you tend to ask more questions and show more personality, both of which lead to greater discovery and deeper relationships.

MUST DO: GET EXPERIENCE WHEN YOU HAVE NO EXPERIENCE

How annoying is it when people say, "Oh I'm sorry but we need someone with experience." *DUH.* As if an employer would ever readily seek out an employee who is clueless to the job at hand. But we all know you have to start somewhere, and sometimes experience can come from a place you least envisioned.

1. Dig deep and find the contact that is closest to what you ultimately want to do, at the company you most want to work for. Once you manage to get that contact info, do NOT use it to ask *how* to get an internship there. You get one chance to make the pitch. Use that opportunity to make a great first impression with a killer cover letter and resumé. I find it lazy when hopefuls email to ask me how to apply to the company. They're basically asking me to do the work for them, and that does not make for a good first impression!

2. No jobs or internships available? Set up exploratory interviews with as many different people as you can. If you're lucky enough to make contact with a person in a company where you'd like to work, you need to milk it for everything.

When you're willing to go on what is essentially a fake interview, you show a lot of enthusiasm and determination. Plus, you can learn a lot from the person you meet. But don't make the mistake of thinking this is a casual chat. **INSIDER TIP: You still need to do the same prep for an exploratory interview that you would do for a legit interview, and you should take it just as seriously, which also means dress appropriately.** Every person you meet gives you the ability to expand your network.

3. At the end of your exploratory interview, ask if it's OK if you stay in touch and inquire about any future positions down the line. Then ask if there's anyone else at the organization that your interviewer might recommend for you to meet, and, if so, politely ask to be introduced. **INSIDER TIP: This question gets your interviewer thinking about YOU and what you want to do. Every supervisor wants to sound knowledgeable, so I'm making a bet that she will come up with other people.**

4. If you can't land an internship at the company of your dreams, you need to make use of your time in other ways. Smaller companies always need help, so it's worth reaching out to them even if you ultimately want to work for a big brand. If you can't afford to quit your day job, perhaps there's a way to work on projects at night or on weekends. It never hurts to ask!! Anything you can do to gain experience and show your determination is worth your time. I know people who have continued projects on their own accord, even after they have left an internship, because they want to keep that connection going.

5. If you still feel like you're getting nowhere, continue learning! The Internet has a wealth of online classes and tutorials

from very established people who can virtually mentor you. If you search your field of interest and add words like "how to" or "IndustryX 101," you would be amazed at how many free tutorials and blogs are dedicated to educating people. You can hone your skills by creating specific searches related to every aspect of the job you want. For example, if I Google "PR 101," over ninety-seven million articles pop up. I could refine the search even more to take a deeper dive, but you get the point. Bottom line, don't wait to be taught; go out and teach yourself. Showing potential employers all the classes you have taken to improve your knowledge will show determination.

Getting your foot in the door takes a lot of work. When I applied for my internship, I didn't have anyone to guide me. I knew that I had to do the work. However, if you're lucky enough to have a lead, you should of course use it to help you break in. That said though, you need to be careful as to how you use your connection. My friend Samantha once shared a cautionary tale with me about a college student trying to get her first job—and relying on her mother to do the heavy lifting. **INSIDER TIP: If you want a profession, you need to act like a professional.**

One day at work, Samantha received a surprising phone call.

"Hi, Samantha, this is Sally, I spoke to you a few years ago about x, y and z."

Samantha had no clue what Sally was talking about.

"Sally, how can I help you?" Samantha asked.

"My daughter is graduating in May and she's looking for a job. She would love the opportunity to work in your department."

Samantha's instinctive thought was, *Why am I talking to you and not her? This girl's mom is calling to get her a job? Was her mom planning to come to the first day of work, too?!* She had to hold herself back from saying, "Your daughter is too old to have Mommy come calling." Instead, Samantha politely explained to Sally that there were no positions available, but Sally pressed on. Samantha was dying to tell this woman to stop ruining her daughter's career, and then she contemplated asking to speak to Sally's daughter so she could school her as well.

Sally was relentless. She wasn't willing to take no for an answer. Every time Samantha tried to end the conversation, Sally suggested another way that she thought her daughter could fit in the department. Samantha ended up having a fifteen-minute conversation with Sally, giving her real advice and information. When she finally got off the phone, Samantha's colleagues flew into her office with "WHO WAS THAT?! That sounded painful!!" Umm yes, it was, and Samantha was thankful to be off the phone.

The next day, Samantha was scrolling through email, when she suddenly saw Sally's name. She was shocked that Sally had made contact again and immediately forwarded it to her team (and eventually me) so that they could share in her amazement. When I read this email myself, I couldn't believe how clueless this mother was. Samantha, of course, agreed with me and was kind enough to share her witty commentary in italicized parentheses.

From: Sally Jones
To: Samantha McNally
Subject: Job for my daughter

Hi Samantha,

I left you a phone message and hope you remember we spoke yesterday. *(No, I forgot, sorry, I have amnesia.)*

My daughter is very interested in the field of communications and reminded me that she was president of the Debate team in High school. *(Totally unrelated and P.S. "debate" and "high" are not proper nouns.)*

I contacted you, because you helped me in the past. *(I'm sorry, but I have no idea who you are, lady.)*

My daughter is looking for a full-time position and would love to work at your company. You directed her to look at your website to see what departments she would be interested in and she is very open and interested in communications. *(I'm still confused as to why I am speaking to you and not her?)*

I am proud to say that my daughter is very smart and is graduating early. *(Umm she's not that smart if she has you calling for her.)* She has had wonderful internships for the past two summers and you can see more information about her on her resumé, which is attached.

She will be living in NY this coming year. She noticed on your website that most positions require working experience.

Everyone needs to begin somewhere. *(Yes, but that's precisely why she should have called me.)* We are hoping she can begin her career with you. We are hoping you can open the door to an interview.

I would so appreciate if you could send her resumé to whoever is in charge of hiring or training programs.

Best Regards,

Sally *(You mean "Mommy")*

Sally was trying to do everything to make sure her daughter didn't fail. She's not a bad parent; it's just that she doesn't realize that she is doing her daughter a disservice. On the reverse side, her daughter doesn't realize how bad it looks to an employer that she isn't doing the outreach herself. To be clear, I am going on the assumption that the daughter knew what her mother was doing. I imagine the conversation going something like: "Honey, I know someone at CompanyX! I will call for you." "Thanks, Mom! That's great!"

But what should have happened is an email like this:

From: Ruby Jones
To: Samantha McNally
Subject: Job Inquiry

Dear Samantha,

I am reaching out to inquire about a position you may have available within your communications department. I have grown up loving your company as my mother knows you from x, y and z. You might recall her? Her name is _____.

(and so on. . . .)

That is a cover letter intro that Samantha would have respected. It's perfectly fine and smart to use any connection you may have to a potential employer, but at a certain point it becomes poor form to not speak for yourself. Having Mommy do the legwork comes off as lazy. Now you may be sitting there blaming the mom, but if that were my mom, I can assure you that I would have never let her call a prospective employer.

It would have been easy to just never reply to Sally's email, but Samantha couldn't sit back and let this scenario ever happen again. She had to educate them; as painful as it was to address it with Sally, she felt she had a responsibility to do so. Samantha sent the following email back:

> From: Samantha McNally
> To: Sally Jones
> Subject: Re: Job for my daughter
>
> Dear Sally,
>   Your daughter should feel free to send her
> resume to PersonX in human resources, but I
> have to tell you that I believe you are doing
> a disservice to her. I am sure you are a
> great mom and one who obviously cares deeply
> about your daughter's success, but by doing
> the work for her, you are actually hurting
> her. She must do the outreach to companies
> herself. I hope you understand my point of
> view and I wish her luck in her job search.
>   Best Regards,
>   Samantha

Then she waited for the explosion. But guess what? Sally was surprisingly appreciative of Samantha's email. Sally responded by explaining that her aim was to make the connection for her daughter through "their" relationship. Samantha explained to Sally that her daughter could have essentially made the same connection herself in her cover letter. Samantha felt really good that she broached the topic with her and genuinely hoped that she made a difference in her daughter's path toward a profession.

A few weeks later, Sally's daughter finally called Samantha herself to inquire about a possible position. Funny thing, she never mentioned her mother or any previous conversations had. Good for her; let bygones be bygones. Better late than never! I love a happy ending, don't you? Three cheers for honesty!

So what can we learn from all of this? Getting experience when you have no experience is not easy and it takes creativity and passion. You absolutely need to use whatever resources are available to you, but you always need to remember the impression that you are trying to make. It's not enough to nail the cover letter and have a good resumé. You also need to act the part. You need to be a professional before you actually are a professional. If you're asking an employer to consider you for a job, you need to show that employer that you are first and foremost taking responsibility for yourself. After all, if you can't be responsible for yourself, how can you possibly handle the job?

CHAPTER THREE

Writing a Killer Cover Letter and Rock-Solid Resumé

THE POSTCOLLEGIATE, RITE-OF-PASSAGE TRIP TO EUROPE WAS AND STILL IS WHAT EVERY COLLEGE GRADUATE THINKS THEY DESERVE. BUT I'VE NEVER been one for roughing it, so deciding to skip backpacking across a continent and sleeping in youth hostels was a very easy decision for me. I also knew that I didn't have a "right" to go. Sure, my internship at *DC Moment* had been great, but it was not nearly enough. One internship does not make an impressive resumé and mine still glaringly lacked fashion experience. I knew I couldn't waste the summer playing; if I wanted to get a job in fashion, I had to buckle down. It was time for *actual* fashion experience. Although none of the lovely people I'd met at *DC Moment* had any connections I could use, I did get one particular nugget of information that I was able to run with. John explained to me that group-publishing companies owned the big fashion magazines. I had never heard of Condé Nast or Hearst before, and that little fact opened my eyes to another world of places I could apply to. See, you never know what you can learn from an experience! Armed with more knowledge than I started with at *DC Moment*, I went back to the newsstand again.

This time I purchased my favorite high-fashion magazines. Those magazines were the ones that I used to wallpaper my room with back in the day, and now they were where I wanted to work. Nothing like aiming high! So I sent my pre-med resumé, now with at least one internship's worth of magazine experience, to the fashion and accessories editors at each of those titles. Just by reading the mastheads, I'd figured out that fashion was somehow a separate department from accessories. I didn't know what the different jobs entailed, but I did know that reaching out to both would increase my odds. I also sent my resumé to the human resources departments at Condé Nast and Hearst, specifying the magazines I was interested in working at.

My cover letter—which I sent to each magazine editor, changing only their names and the name of the magazine—was as sincere as I could make it without being nauseating. I also geared it toward the fashion-conscious. If I was emailing multiple people at the same magazine, I made sure to alter each letter so that they wouldn't be identical.

Dear Mr. Johnson,

My name is Aliza Bernfeld and I am a senior at the University of Maryland. I'm currently a neurobiology and physiology major and I have been working toward becoming a plastic surgeon since high school. But this past summer when I interned at a local hospital, I came to the harsh realization that my passion for medicine was no longer there. Upon further reflection, I recognized that my childhood love for fashion has never really gone away. You see, I grew up with Haute's fashion pages on my bedroom walls, and fashion has always inspired me. But ironically, as much as I love fashion, I never understood that fashion was a career that I could pursue.

I decided to take steps to better understand the magazine industry in the hopes that my experience would lead me to an internship at Haute Magazine. Working at DC Moment showed me that I am extremely interested in the editorial side of a magazine. I hope that you will allow me the privilege of learning how your magazine is created this summer. Enclosed, please find my resumé for your perusal.

Thank you in advance for your consideration.

Sincerely,
Aliza Bernfeld

I concluded that I had nothing to lose by telling the truth. Yes, I'd made a mistake, but with the help of these editors, I was very much hoping to correct it. I've always been a very forthright person, and I think that has helped me gain the trust of many. I believe that there is something very attractive about honesty. **INSIDER TIP: When you have a glaring omission or lack of experience on your resumé, it's best to address it head-on.**

My letter to *Haute Magazine* worked, and I received an offer to join their team as an intern in the accessories department. My dream came true!

MUST DO: WRITE A KILLER COVER LETTER

There are thousands of books out there on how to write a cover letter. I haven't read a single one. The dos and don'ts that I will share with you are based purely on what I have seen throughout my career. I know which cover letters I react well to and which ones I don't. If you've got the basics down pat, good for you! But I can promise you, based on what I've seen, too many people don't. Plus, it never hurts to be reminded of the 101 stuff, because truly nothing is worse than making a rookie mistake.

1. Spell the name of the person you are addressing correctly. *(You don't deserve employment if you don't!)*
2. Refer to the person by his or her correct professional title, and spell that correctly, too. Don't you dare think to yourself that you can't find this. If it's not readily available on the Internet, make a phone call. **INSIDER TIP: Do not abbreviate! Abbreviating is perceived as both casual and lazy.**
3. Spell the company's name correctly. (I can't tell you how many times I've seen "passionate fans of the brand" spell the company's name wrong on a cover letter. Seriously? I have no words.) Oh and P.S. consult the company's official website. **INSIDER TIP: Google searches will pull anything, including user-generated content with incorrect spellings! Google is not official; neither is Wikipedia.**
4. Use formal writing etiquette. That means NO text-message speak. *(You are NOT friends!)* Dust off "Dear" and "Sincerely," because you'll need them.
5. Choose your font carefully. For professional correspondence I like Arial. For a more personal, less formal letter, I

love Century Gothic. Please, *please* do not send your cover letter in Comic Sans (puke!) or any other font with too much personality. Your font should match the industry you are applying for. For example, Times New Roman for a position at a law firm would probably be the right call.

6. Use a font size no bigger than 10. The bigger your font, the more casual your writing will seem. A smaller font shows the letter's recipient that you understand professional correspondence and you're keeping yourself in check.

7. Do not write in all caps, because that's considered SCREAMING. When people write in all caps I can feel my hair blowing back!

8. Do not use exclamation points. The tone of the letter should be professional, not *squeeeel!!!*

9. Do not use any punctuation that would be interpreted as chummy or overly comfortable. Emoticons (like smiley faces, for example) are unacceptable in any professional correspondence when you have yet to form a close working relationship. So are abbreviations like LOL, IRL, etc. Even little marks that denote friendliness should be avoided. For example, a lot of people in the fashion world sign off with a kiss on email like this:

   Aliza x

   You do not do that when you don't know the person reading your letter. You especially don't do that when you are applying for a job. Just remember that when trying to impress a potential employer, casual correspondence kills. K?

10. If someone has recommended that you contact the person you're writing, always mention that right at the start of your cover letter. For example:

> Dear Jane,
>
> John Doe suggested that I reach out to you regarding the manager position available in your department.

It goes without saying that John Doe better have really recommended you do that. Never name-drop for the sake of name-dropping. It never ends well!

11. Include one or two sentences that summarize who you are and what you've been doing professionally. Remember that these sentences should relate back to the job at hand. You must focus on getting the employer's attention. But be brief! This is the part where you have to choose between your babies (a.k.a. the most important pieces of yourself). If it helps, pretend that you're on a morning show and the news anchor has asked you to describe yourself in six seconds before they go to commercial break. What would be the most important statement you would make?

12. Include at least one really good line conveying why you want to work at that specific company. It's not enough to say you want to work "in communications," for example. Prove why you want to work in communications *there*. **INSIDER TIP: It's really ALL about them.**

13. If you can, cite one of the company's recent accomplishments that you really admire. That shows that you are really up on the company and a true fan. Even if you're not, fake it, baby.

14. Get to the point quickly. Nothing is worse than a person taking forever to get to the punch line.

15. Read it over multiple times. Seriously.

16. The last time, read it backward. Yup, you heard me. When you read copy backward, you inevitably read more slowly,

which is a great way to catch spelling, punctuation or grammar errors that you might otherwise blow past.

17. If you are emailing this correspondence, the cover letter should be written right into the body of the email with the resumé document attached. People are lazy, and opening two attachments is one more step they might not want to take.

18. Or better yet, GPS your resumé! Upload it to a "share file" system. This way, you can track when your document has been downloaded or the link to your file has been shared. Your cover letter should be written right into the body of the email inviting the recipient to download your resumé.

19. Don't include promises like, "I will call you next week to follow up." Because a) that just solidifies the fact that this employer need not take any action, since you've promised to do the following up, and b) what if for some reason you forget to do it? You're setting yourself up for failure either way.

20. Close the letter thanking the recipient "in advance" for her consideration. I like this for good measure, as it doesn't actually do anything in particular except make for a nice ending.

I didn't have very much to put on my resumé at this stage in my journey toward fashion, but what I didn't want to do was mess up all my hard work on a penalty for stupid fonts, poor wording or lack of maturity. The key to a good resumé is to include the content that will be relevant to the employer or position you are going for. For example, being in charge of the office supply closet does not impress me. That's not a marketable skill. But if you told me that you were able to reduce the monthly office supply bill by 15 percent by reorganizing the way supplies were distributed, that's something I would be impressed to see. You have to focus on skills that an employer reading your resumé would see value in. What experience do you have that can be an asset to this position? You don't have to list everything. For example, I don't care what sorority or fraternity you were in. I want to know what you did in college that is going to help the company. So if you were president or social chair of that sorority, that tells me something. It tells me that when you speak, people listen. That's a skill worth sharing. If you can answer, "Why would they care about this?" to every bullet point you write, you're in good shape. If you can't, lose it.

MUST DO: WRITE A KILLER RESUMÉ

I've reviewed hundreds of resumés and whenever I do, it takes me about a nanosecond to decipher if it's going in the trash or not. If I boot a resumé out of the game right away, it's because the writer was sloppy and messed up the basics. So I'm going to go ahead and go over the rudimentary things that everyone should know, because based on what I see, they don't.

Once you have the foundation, you need to make sure your resumé style matches the job you are applying for. If you are applying to be the executive assistant to a CEO in finance, then perhaps your lavender resumé paper and swirly, scripted font might be better suited to a bridal shower invitation. I'm a very visual person, so paper color, quality and font inevitably make a powerful first impression. When you design your resumé, you need to always remember that this little piece of paper is the only thing representing you until you hopefully get called in to interview. So what do you want to show that employer?

1. Start with your objective and tailor it very specifically to the job you are applying for. That means you might have multiple versions of your resumé for multiple job applications. Keep the wording brief and to the point. (For example, if you are applying for a job in public relations, but include an objective about wanting to work in marketing, that is going to show your potential employer that a) you don't know the difference or b) you were not careful when you re-edited your resumé for multiple positions.)

   Here are a few examples of objectives for a candidate pursuing a job in PR, but applying to various companies:

   Objective: To secure a position in the public relations department at a luxury fashion brand.
   Objective: To secure a position in the public relations department of a fashion magazine.
   Objective: To secure a position as an account manager at a public relations agency specializing in fashion.

   All three of these objectives show this person wants to work in PR, but it specifies *where* they want to work in PR. As I've stated previously, one size does not fit all!
2. Every company you've worked for should be listed formally (no abbreviations), with the exact title of the position you held.
3. Under each position title, list your job accomplishments, not only your responsibilities. **INSIDER TIP: What you have done is more important than what you were supposed to do.**
4. Do try to apply statistical information to each accomplishment. For example, it's not enough to say that you "grew the business." You need to be specific and say, for example, that you "grew the business by 5 percent."

5. Do not list accomplishments that are clearly the work of the team. For example, if you were an intern and you state that you secured three new clients for the firm, I'm not going to believe that. **INSIDER TIP: Keep your resumé real, otherwise people will see right through you.**

6. List the dates of employment for each job. List your most recent and relevant experience first.

7. Describe your skills in the most sophisticated way you can. For example, don't just state that you're "social savvy." Instead, state that you are social media trained with specific knowledge of x, y and z platforms and grew a community of x number of fans.

8. Include multiple ways for an employer to contact you. These ways should also be the best ways. For example, if you know you can never talk at work, then why list your work phone number? Include the contact information that you know you have the most access to, because you're going to want to respond quickly. Taking four days to return a phone call from a potential employer is not a good look. If you want to include your social profiles, you should include them at the bottom as a separate line item since you obviously don't want a potential employer contacting you publicly for the world to see!

9. But before you include your social media profiles, make sure that you are comfortable with what an employer might find if they searched them. If you're not, make them private or delete any questionable posts.

10. Use the same type of keywords that the employer might list in a job search profile. Don't make them have to think! Make it easy. For example, if the employer includes technical skill terms on the job posting, serve them right back up on your cover letter.

11. If you have gaps of time in your job history, it is best to address what you were doing during that time. Try to phrase the language to be as favorable as possible to the job you are applying for. For example, if you took time off to travel to India, explain what you got out of that experience that could possibly add value to your next endeavor. No matter what, though: account for the time.
12. It is OK to omit unimportant experiences or jobs if they are not going to enhance your resumé, but only if omitting them does not create new gaps of time.

You never get a second chance to make a first impression, and that is how you have to think of your cover letter and resumé. They are taking you on your first date. But just like in the early stages of dating, you need to bring your A-game every time. These documents are never final. They need to be reviewed with fine scrutiny every time, before you send them out again. I promise you that with every review you will find a typo or an opportunity to make a bullet point better. Sometimes you might even find something that you can't believe you included! Looking at your cover letter and resumé anew is even more important if some time has passed since the last time you sent them out. When you view these documents with fresh eyes, you are giving yourself a chance to reconsider how you might be perceived. Most importantly, though, make sure your current documents make sense for this new potential job opportunity.

CHAPTER FOUR

Sucking Your Internship Dry

I REMEMBER MY MOTHER DRIVING ME INTO NEW YORK CITY ON THE FIRST DAY OF MY *HAUTE* INTERNSHIP. I DIDN'T KNOW WHAT TO WEAR OR HOW TO act—but it turned out that didn't really matter, because I was the last person anybody there was thinking about. If people even looked in my direction and blinked at me, I was lucky. But that was also fortunate, because this anonymity gave me a chance to take in my surroundings and absorb the way things were done: how people dressed, what they sounded like, who was friends with whom, etc. My boss was a very dynamic guy named Dean Johnson who was handsome in a boyish way with wavy brown hair and the most endearing smile. He'd been at *Haute Magazine* for many years, and I could immediately tell that he was very well liked and great at what he did. His team consisted of two women named Cara and Meredith. Cara was the more senior editor of the two, and she had that olive-skinned, "I just came back from vacation" look going for her. She also had an equally relaxed disposition, which made working for her a nice experience. Meredith was a born-and-bred

New Yorker, one whose wit was as sharp as her heels were high. Meredith kept the day lively and made the office a fun place to be. The three of them seemed to get along famously, creating a work environment that was both entertaining and interesting. They were my first teachers in what would be my very long education in the fashion industry.

Dean's job was to edit the accessories collections and decide the trends based on what he thought was relevant to the *Haute Magazine* reader. He curated accessories for his own "still-life" pages and provided accessories options to the fashion department for whatever model shoots they were styling. He would present his ideas for all of this in "run-throughs" with the editor in chief or the fashion director, and they would decide what would ultimately go on the shoot. At *Haute* I learned that just because something goes on a photo shoot, doesn't mean it actually gets photographed. I also learned that just because something gets photographed, doesn't mean the image is going to turn out great, in which case it gets dropped from the story.

There was an extraordinary amount of product that needed to be "called in" for shoots. Cara and Meredith had relationships with the in-house public relations people at all the major design houses as well as outside PR agencies that represented various designers. Essentially, they would call in product for the magazine to borrow for a short period of time, and then the product would be returned to its rightful home. It was the job of the interns—a.k.a. me—to "check in" the product, which meant taking a Polaroid (yes, a Polaroid, on film) of every single accessory and documenting the date it arrived and the date it was returned. This inventory process was tedious, but essential. Designers sometimes produce only one sample of an item. That one sample needs to be loaned out for hundreds of photo shoots around the world.

If Cara requested a Prada bag for a photo shoot, the PR person she called might tell her:

a) That it's available from x date to y date
b) That it's not available because it's out on another shoot (the name of the other magazine never being disclosed)
c) That it's not available because it's out with CelebX (name definitely disclosed for effect)
d) That it's out for a sales event (usually a lie and the real answer is b)

So if Cara was lucky enough to get a coveted handbag in for Dean, I can promise you that there was a very specific "return date" that had to be honored. If we messed up and caused the item to miss the next shoot on the PR person's schedule, she might never loan us her precious samples again.

For the duration of an accessory's stay at *Haute Magazine*, it would reside in the closet. The closet was essentially a large room filled with racks, shelves and hooks. But what filled those racks and shelves were thousands of dollars of designer accessories. Every luxury designer you could ever imagine was represented. We had hundreds of shoes, handbags and trays of costume jewelry, hats, scarves and belts. It was any girl's dream closet and of course it was the place that I loved the most at the magazine. It was my job to maintain the closet, making sure the shoes were all properly arranged by color and style, the bag styles were kept together, the belts were hung and the jewelry was perfectly placed on velvet trays. I was also a self-appointed Chief Bunny Collector, picking out the dust bunnies that would inexplicably, yet inevitably, accumulate on a daily basis.

The thing about getting your first big break is, you have to be enamored with everything. I was the first person to turn on the lights at the office in the morning and usually the last person to leave. I never sat around idle. I always asked if there was something else I should be doing. I thought ahead and would try to take the next logical step so that when Dean asked me to do something, I could happily say that it was already done. **INSIDER TIP: Anticipate your boss's needs.** I absorbed. I asked questions. I didn't waste a minute of time but instead always tried to learn something new. I was business-focused.

A great attitude is one of your most marketable skills, and if you can muster the energy and passion to have a good attitude about any task, large or small, then you will get very far. You can always tell when an employee thinks, "Oh, that's stupid. I'm not going to put a lot of effort into that." Wrong attitude! You have to think about how that task serves the bigger picture. Every job matters along the food chain, so take pride in everything you do, even if it seems pointless at the time. Also, if you throw a fit when you have to do something you don't want to, I can promise you that when a good project pops up, it will be given to someone else.

So I embraced every aspect of my internship, and with every day that passed, I started to get more comfortable with the people I worked with. Dean and the girls were so warm and friendly that it was easy for me to begin to feel like I was truly part of the team. One day, I decided to ask the question that had been on my mind since day one.

"How did I get this internship? I'm just curious because I didn't exactly have the right experience," I asked Dean.

Dean threw me a sassy look from across the room and said, "Honey, that's exactly why we liked you! You had a different perspective. You don't need to have fashion experience to love fashion. And your cover letter rocked."

There you have it. Honesty had worked, and in this case, my lack of a fashion major hadn't mattered.

From that moment on, I felt an even greater sense of belonging, but I still minded my behavior. If they were serious, I was. If they were playful, so was I, although I made sure never to come across as *more* playful than they did. **INSIDER TIP: Calibrate your behavior based on your boss's cues.** In the beginning, you never want to play or laugh too hard because when you do, it reminds your superiors that you're only an intern, and a way-too-comfortable one at that. The trick is to be aware of people's reactions. A good stand-up comedian always knows when he has lost the audience. You have to pay attention to the reaction you get when you're putting yourself out there a bit more loudly. If it's an awkward one, pull back accordingly.

Even though I was feeling comfortable and liked, I still knew there were limits. The editors often borrowed accessories from the closet if they were running out to an important appointment or out for an evening event. The closet was essentially their closet. I could see how after a while, you definitely start to feel like those accessories are yours. But that perk was not something I would dare ask for.

One day I was in the closet holding a pair of amazing Mary Jane stacked heel pumps. I'm not going to lie; I was fantasizing about how great they would look with my outfit and imagined myself wearing them after work at

Bryant Park, where I was going for drinks that night. At that moment, Meredith came in and somehow knew exactly what I was thinking.

"Do you want to borrow them?" she asked.

"Oh, no, I couldn't," I said, totally unconvincingly.

"Sure you can!" she replied. "Enjoy them. Just bring them back tomorrow."

Ahhhhh!!! I can't even express the excitement I felt. Not only because I got to wear killer heels, but even more so, because Meredith had trusted me. I was really becoming one of them.

I wore the Mary Jane pumps to drinks that night and was the envy of all of my friends. Hell, I was practically envious of *myself*. I felt like a million bucks. It was in that moment that I really felt the power of fashion, how a great shoe or dress or accessory can change your mind-set and boost your confidence. As long as those shoes were on my feet I felt unstoppable. P.S. I would later go on to buy those same shoes at a sample sale and have a near-death experience in them when the heel broke off midstride on Madison Avenue. No big deal (*S).

Getting around in high heels was a must-have skill for every editor. In fact, at the time, there was many a rumor that fashion editors at certain high-profile magazines were actually not allowed to wear flats. Well, thankfully, as an intern who had to run around like crazy, no one cared if I did.

One stormy afternoon I was asked to run an errand. "Aliza, can you rush-deliver this hosiery to the set at Lincoln Center? It's really urgent, so take a cab," one of the editors instructed me. I rushed out of the office with no raincoat and no umbrella. Of course, on a rainy afternoon in New

York City, you could more easily win the lottery than find an available cab, so I had to take the subway. By the time I arrived at Lincoln Center and had made my way across its vast open courtyard, I was soaked to the bone, but I didn't care. I was going to save the day on the shoot! I ran into the building like I was delivering a live heart to a transplant surgeon and my arrival would literally save lives. "These are for you, Paul," I said breathlessly to the on-set assistant as he snatched the bag from my hands and walked off.

And that was it. No marching band of thanks for me. No "You saved the day, Aliza!" I don't know why I expected so much more gratitude, but I realized on that day it would be a long time before someone appreciated something I did. "Thank you," it seemed, was not in most fashion people's vocabularies. **INSIDER TIP: Don't expect a thank-you or a pat on the back. Do a great job for YOURSELF.**

I returned to the office a bit defeated, but mostly thrilled to have witnessed a real photo shoot, if only for a moment. So what if I was a glorified messenger? One day, you're hobnobbing in Bryant Park in designer shoes, and the next, you're a rain-soaked minion who didn't get a "thanks." All that mattered was that one day I would play a more meaningful role. **INSIDER TIP: Put your head down and just do the work.**

After a couple of successful months at *Haute Magazine*, I decided that maybe it was also a good idea to get more fashion experience to put on my resumé. I asked Dean if it would be OK to cut my days down to four so that I could also intern somewhere else. He was amenable. Please note that I would have never even broached this idea had I not been confident that I had invested enough solid time at *Haute* and had proven myself to Dean. I knew that I would have his support because he knew I was a hardworking and dedicated intern. I knew he would understand what I was trying to do.

Another *Haute* fashion editor got wind that I was looking for an additional internship opportunity and mentioned that her cousin was the fashion director at *Le Ville Magazine* and that maybe they needed some interns. She called her cousin and arranged a phone interview for me. Shoot, score! I got the one-day-a-week gig. Friday would be my day of the week to go to *Le Ville* and hopefully learn more applicable skills. But most importantly, I would be able to get my second "fashion bullet point" to put on my resumé.

If *Haute* was the angel of internships, *Le Ville* turned out to be the devil. First off, *Le Ville* wasn't technically a fashion magazine, so the makeshift fashion department was confined to the magazine's tiny floral-and-mahogany-decorated conference room. (Seriously, I can't think of a decor less fashionable.) There was an army of us, which was good because there's always safety in numbers, but there wasn't enough room for everyone. The hours we worked, meanwhile, were completely insane. Sometimes we would stay in that one room until two in the morning, packing up for shoots.

On top of those subpar working conditions, the fashion editor, Leanne, was a total nightmare. (P.S. the fashion director, a.k.a. the cousin of the *Haute* fashion editor who recommended me, was lovely and not the issue. The problem was that she was often out of the office on shoots and we were left with Leanne.) She pretty much treated us like dirt—never actually talking to us, just spitting out orders. It was at *Le Ville Magazine* that I learned a valuable lesson: how *not* to be. It's funny; sometimes you learn the most from watching people display their worst.

I had been lucky to have nurturing bosses at *Haute*, so this was new for me. But at the end of the day, I just needed to put *Le Ville Magazine* on my resumé and hopefully get a glowing reference letter out of it as well. **INSIDER TIP: Suck it up and get the most out of the experience, no matter what.**

After five months of interning, I had finally made a career dent. So when an accessories assistant position opened up at *Atelier Magazine*, Dean recommended me for the job. Actually, he pretty much threatened the *Atelier* team that if they didn't hire me, he'd kill them. I am forever indebted to Dean; he was the fairy godfather that everyone needs at one point or another to break through.

There's always that one person who gives you the chance, who takes you under his wing and changes your career path forever. If you can identify a supervisor with a generous teaching spirit, then it's worth your time and energy to make sure you continue to cultivate that relationship. Unfortunately, it's easy to lose touch with people as you move around in business, but if you make an effort to keep going back to the well, you will begin to create that mentor/ mentee relationship. Be sure to keep your mentor abreast of where you are and how things are going. If you are contemplating a move, your mentor is the perfect person to bounce opportunities past. When you have implemented some of his advice and the results have been favorable, let your mentor know. He will be thrilled he was right and able to help! You should be sure to always thank your mentor for all his support. A handwritten note goes a long way. From time to time, you could also send a token of thanks, like flowers. These little gestures show that you value the advice given and the time your mentor has taken to show you the way. These relationships are essential to nurture early, as they will prove invaluable to you as you move up your career ladder. **INSIDER TIP: Find a mentor or career angel to build a strategic and meaningful professional relationship with.**

MUST DO: INTERN LIKE A ROCK STAR

When you enter a real work environment for the first time, especially as a college student starting an internship, remember why you want to be there: First and foremost, to learn real marketable skills that can enhance your resumé and to secure a strong referral from your supervisor. You do not go about getting these things by thinking, "Oh, I'm just an intern, so this experience doesn't really matter." Too many people make the mistake of thinking that since they don't "really" work somewhere, how they present themselves isn't of consequence. On the contrary, how you present yourself matters more because you're trying to prove yourself and break in.

By the last day of your internship, your boss should be begging for you to stay. She should be saying things like, "What are we going to do without you?" *That* is a lasting impression. *That* is a reference nailed. Here's how you do that:

1. Dress the part: The more you can dress to fit the office culture, the easier it will be for people there to visualize you as part of the team. Now, here's where you start panicking that you don't have the money to shop for new clothes. Listen: Shop thrift stores or borrow from friends. When my sister and I get bored of our closets we swap wardrobes. It feels as gratifying as shopping! If you can afford to, invest in accessories. A quality shoe or handbag is much harder to fake. When in doubt about your wardrobe, wear black.

Black doesn't make mistakes. Be mindful of the cuts: The office is no place for strapless or cleavage. Miniskirts can also be a no-no. You're not stupid so you don't need me to tell you this but...don't dress like you're going out clubbing. Guys, for you the advice is different. For some reason, men underestimate the importance of a clean, pressed shirt. Don't dress like you've just rolled out of bed. A sleepy outfit can give the impression of a sleepy mind.

2. Investigate your employers beforehand: Google the names of anyone you know who works there. Study them and memorize who they are. There's no excuse for not knowing who the CEO of a company is—when you end up in the elevator alone with him, you don't want to mistakenly ignore him. If you can, it's also smart to examine your future coworkers' body language in photographs; are they really smiley and having fun or are they serious and stiff? If they've been quoted anywhere, what did they say? What do people say about them? Think like an investigative reporter and come up with a few takeaways as to what the tone of the office might be like. **INSIDER TIP: Know the players or you won't know how to play the game.**

3. Be on time: No, better yet, get there before everyone else does. If your boss shows up and you're already in the office, that's bonus points and if you ask your supervisor the night before what project you could start in the morning, you'll achieve rock star status in no time. Going above and beyond will pay off, I promise you. And if you have the nerve to be late, guess what you're giving off? The "I don't really value this opportunity" sign. You may as well pick out your tombstone now, because, honey, you are dead and buried.

4. Remember, you're not one of them: You don't actually have a job, you have an internship. Your boss doesn't want to

hear unsolicited information about your boyfriend problems or what you ate for dinner last night, and she certainly doesn't want to hear that you're so tired because you were out partying until three a.m. On the flip side, your boss doesn't want to be interrogated by you either. Don't ask personal questions. You'll know if and when the relationship evolves because she'll start voluntarily disclosing personal tidbits about her life. Even then, you're better off as the listener than the blabbermouth. It should not be you sending the first "we're friends now" signal. **INSIDER TIP: Filter what you say to your boss.**

5. Learn to self-start: Not every manager is good at delegating and giving direction, so taking the initiative to make your own work goes a long way. Nothing is worse than seeing an intern sitting around because he has nothing to do. If you can't figure out what you should or could be doing, then by all means, ask.

6. Take a hint: When you start working in an office, you need to pay close attention to the culture and the atmosphere. Is it loud? Is it serious? Are people eating lunch at their desks? You know what they say, when in Rome . . . same idea here. You need to follow the lead of the environment and try to mimic the way your colleagues work. If everyone wears black daily and you decide you're going to wear red, you're making a very loud statement and not necessarily a positive one. Best to wait until you have really established yourself.

7. Don't question everything: Whoever said, "There are no stupid questions," was wrong. That said, do your boss a favor and try to research the answers to your own questions before you ask them. I would much rather someone say, "The Condé Nast building is at One World Trade Center.

I just wanted to check that's where you want the package sent," as opposed to, "Where is the Condé Nast building?"

8. Don't gossip: Once you spend enough time in an office, you'll start to realize that office politics are a lot like high school; word travels fast through the hallways. Don't add to the fodder. Keep your mouth shut and don't weigh in on issues that have nothing to do with you. That also goes for what you say outside the office. Everyone loves to tell the story that begins, "My friend who interns at CompanyX heard . . ." Eventually though, the people who work at CompanyX get wind of it. It's a small world out there.

9. Yes, yes, yes and also yes: When it comes to work-related tasks, the only word you know is "yes." And not yes with an attitude, a sigh or an eye roll. It's "Yes!!" with bells on. Managers should not be made to feel like they're putting you out by asking you to do something, and saying "yes" when your body language is saying "don't bother me!" is not good interning strategy. Of course, if you're ever asked to do something that makes you feel uncomfortable, by all means do not do it. No job is worth sacrificing your values or morals. You'll know where to draw the line.

10. Don't be a zombie: Silence can mistakenly come off as rudeness. If you see a colleague, say hello! If you have nothing to do, ask for an assignment. Be a self-starter. Be responsive to instructions. I understand that it can be intimidating, but the more conversation you have with your supervisor, the more impact you will make.

11. Don't go above heads: It's natural to want time with the big boss, but your direct supervisor is the one you need to make happy. If she sees that you're not so enamored of her, but you're ass-kissing her boss, she's not going to be pleased.

The hierarchy in a department is very important and people take it seriously. You should, too.

12. Social media: It's tempting to post on social media as the day goes on, but focusing on your job is a better idea. Remember that people can see what you post! You definitely don't want to give off the impression that you're not taking work seriously. You also don't want to look like your mind is elsewhere, or worse, get caught talking about your colleagues (even anonymously) behind their backs. It goes without saying, but I'll say it just in case: Don't post about your internship! What happens in the office stays in the office. **INSIDER TIP: Read the company's social media policy before posting anything—even after hours.**

I will go into a lot of detail about social media later in this book, but since this topic is so important to your professional life, it's worth mentioning this here as well.

Think about it this way: You are trying to create a reputation for yourself in the workplace, so don't endanger that reputation by being unprofessional on your personal platforms. **INSIDER TIP: You don't want your social media profile to give off a negative impression and influence the people you work with in the wrong way.**

A few quick rules:
- Don't follow or friend your internship supervisor. You can consider doing so after the internship is over when you know that you have established a good relationship.
- Same goes for LinkedIn! Your supervisor does not want to connect with you, because she doesn't even know you or how you work. Wait until after the internship, when you have proven yourself.
- If your supervisor follows or friends you first, you should reciprocate, but don't engage with her unless spoken to

first. I know you're thinking that I'm being a stickler, and why not try to build a relationship via social? I promise you that it will be too much, too soon.

- If you are connected through social media, then you better take extra care to think about what you are posting before you post it. This may feel stifling, but you have to suck that up. Though these are your personal social media profiles, there are rules.

Before you get the internship, however, using social media to connect with companies or executives is a great way to network. In fact, I would highly recommend it. I have met many students through social media who have secured internships and even jobs through social connections. Jenna, whom you read about in the introduction of this book, is the best example! But that said, social networking with potential employers is best done prior to securing the internship and after you leave.

13. Take advantage of the team: You have professionals at your fingertips, so don't waste the opportunity to learn about your colleagues and find out how they got started. I'm sure they'll have great stories to tell, and one of them may spark an idea that can help you. It's also smart to ask them every once in a while for feedback on how you're doing. Finding out what you could correct while you still have time to is better than a) never knowing and b) finding out when you're about to leave the internship. You are essentially giving yourself a chance to improve your supervisor's impression of you, so take that opportunity! Constructive criticism will only help you, and it's easier sometimes for your supervisor to give that if she's been directly asked for it.

14. Leave graciously: Don't forget to thank your supervisor for a wonderful experience. **INSIDER TIP: Make sure you thank everyone on the team, not just the most senior person.** If you feel you deserve it, ask if she wouldn't mind being a reference for you. In fact, you can ask anyone on the team that you know you have worked with if she would be a reference. The more the better! Keep a file of your references so that one day, when you need them, you have them at your fingertips. Because people often change jobs, try to get personal contact information as well. Of course you could try to connect on LinkedIn, but sometimes supervisors find this method a bit forward because you want the connection and they might not. Remember that LinkedIn is as much your supervisor's professional network as it is yours.

Just because you get the reference though, doesn't mean that your work is done. As annoying as it is, you will need to reach out to that reference right before you are about to interview for a job and ask again if it would be OK to use her as a reference. I know you're thinking, "But wait, they already said yes and I have the letter to prove it!" I get it. But here's the thing: By re-asking, you are reconnecting with that person and reminding her about who you are and what impression you left. That way, when a potential employer calls, she is prepared. Time will inevitably have passed and managers have countless interns. You don't want to be embarrassed by having the potential employer catch your old supervisor off guard. It's your job to reach out and remind her who you are; hopefully, she will remember you and be willing to speak on your behalf now. It's not a given.

Making the most of an internship is the most important thing you can do when you're starting out. Not only does interning allow you to learn important skills, it provides you with invaluable networking possibilities. Whom you connect with can lead you to your next job. You're also more likely to hear of opportunities when you're in an office and are top of mind. If Dean hadn't recommended me for the job at *Atelier*, I might not have heard about it. If you suck your internship dry and gain the trust of your supervisor, you can continue to use that resource long after you've left. Making sure not to stalk, you can check in with your previous supervisor every once in a while to see if she has heard of any job openings that might be right for you. **INSIDER TIP: People who already have jobs hear about job opportunities first.** If she does and knows the person hiring, then maybe she would be willing to forward along your resumé, too. Remember that people trust people they know. Your performance is the key to getting to that level of trust. So don't blow a great opportunity to make that kind of impact on a supervisor.

CHAPTER FIVE

Nailing Your First Interview

ON DEAN'S GLOWING RECOMMENDATION, I WAS
CALLED IN TO INTERVIEW FOR AN ASSISTANT POSI-
TION IN THE ACCESSORIES DEPARTMENT AT *ATELIER*.
It was my first real job interview and I was petrified. The
only relevant experience I had was my bit of real fashion
experience from *Haute Magazine* and a little bit of *Le Ville*,
and of course the passion for what I'd learned at those
places over the summer.

To prepare, I bought the latest issue of *Atelier Magazine*
and pored over it while trying to understand its point of
view. *Atelier* was a good fashion magazine, but it wasn't as
high fashion as *Haute Magazine*, nor did it even exist when
I was busy wallpapering my bedroom walls in junior high.
I could tell its tone was friendly and informative and it definitely had a large fashion component, but it was not as edgy
as *Haute*.

I went in to meet with the newly promoted accessories
editor, Elizabeth, who had just gotten permission to hire an
assistant. Elizabeth was a tall woman with the palest blond
hair you could ever imagine. She had sharp features and

watery blue eyes. Upon first glance, she seemed intimidating, but when we sat down to talk, she was warm and engaging. I felt an instant connection with her and I hoped that the feeling was mutual. I was pretty sure I would move on to the next round of interviews, this time with the accessories director, Heather.

Heather was short and not as fashion-forward as Elizabeth. In fact, she didn't strike me as someone who would even work in fashion. Her look was simple and classic; she had a short brown pixie cut and wore tortoise glasses. If I were casting her in a film, I would have pegged her for a teacher. But as innocuous as Heather's look was, her interview game wasn't. Something about the way she spoke made me feel like she was trying to purposely trip me up. She asked a lot of questions that mandated subjective answers: What did I think of the magazine? What style of hosiery would I pair with a pencil skirt? What shoe would I style with that skirt and hose? What did I think the magazine could do better? What other magazines did I read? Who were my favorite designers? What was my favorite show from that season? I suspected that the only right answers were the ones she would have come up with. I imagined that she was judging my taste, how quick I was on the draw and how comfortable I was sitting in the hot seat. I walked out of there very unsure about how my answers went over, but I did know that I spoke well and confidently, and I had to assume that would count for something. Well, I guess I was right, because a few days later I was offered the position.

Take a Selfie: Can You Master the Interview?

Interviewing is the worst, isn't it? It's so easy to blow your chances because the audience matters almost as much as you do. Here's the good news though: You are in charge of what comes out of your mouth. One of the biggest mistakes I see people make is that while trying to prove their worth, they use the wrong language and tone. Of course you need to promote your accomplishments, but there is a way to do that. Take a look:

1. Do you sound cocky or confident?

    Cocky: "I'm the best person on my team."
    Confident: "I've been fortunate to have been able to lead a team on several projects this year."
    Cocky: "I can do everything well."
    Confident: "I am an experienced multitasker who works well under pressure."

    Do you see the difference? Cocky is not like-able, but confident can be. A smart person will admire someone who's politely confident, but everyone will hate someone who's cocky. So you need to promote your skills and positive attributes without making the person who's interviewing you hate you. People generally want cocky people to fail. Just remember that.

2. Are you a good communicator of your strengths? You might be great at certain core competencies, but if you can't communicate examples of how

you use those skills well, it will just end up sounding like a lot of noise. Come to the interview with a list of three to five examples where you're showing, not just telling, how well you know your stuff.

3. Are you praising your prospective company's accomplishments? You want to show the person interviewing you that you have been following along, that you're an avid fan of the brand. While you should make sure to reference specific achievements you secretly know your interviewer had a hand in (which you'll know because you'll Google your interviewer beforehand), be wary of obvious ass-kissing here. People can smell that a mile away.

4. Do you maintain eye contact? Do you look and sound interested?

5. Are you showing that you've got the right personality for the job? For example, in public relations you need to have an outgoing personality because the entire job is about your ability to deal with people. If you look like a miserable person with no life to you, I don't care what public relations skills you have, you're not someone I want on my team.

6. Are you prepared to talk about a big obstacle and how you overcame it?

7. Do you have an example ready to demonstrate how you collaborated well with a team?

8. Do you have an answer to the dreaded "What are your weaknesses" question? It's actually a big mistake to answer it a) with complete honesty and/or b) in a way that assumes your interviewer

is a moron. "I take on too much!" is not a weakness. "I don't know how to say no!" is not a weakness. What's worse, these fake answers are insulting to the person interviewing you. So how do you handle it? Try this out for size: "I'm never sure how to answer this question—not because I'm perfect, I'm certainly not—but because I don't feel that there's anything in my skill set that would be a concern in getting this job done well. I truly believe my skills are a great match for this position."

If the interviewer presses you on this, try a diversion. For example: "If I were asked to either do budget allocations or write press releases all day, my best use of time would definitely be writing press releases. I can do budget allocations well enough, but I'm not a lover of numbers." Notice I did not throw back the word "weakness" to the interviewer. "Weakness" is such a negative word that it bears no repeating. Also realize when answering this trick question that you need to keep in mind the job you are applying for. If you're interviewing for a position in an accounting firm, then saying you're not a lover of numbers is probably not a good idea! **INSIDER TIP: Your "weakness" should never be a core competency of the job you're going for.**

9. Are you prepared with questions to ask the interviewer about the company and/or the position you're applying for—questions that you can't find the answers to on the Internet? For example, don't ask the interviewer when the company was

founded, since that is clearly something you could Google in a nanosecond. No one likes their time wasted, but worse, no one likes to waste their time interviewing someone who clearly didn't do his homework. Some examples of smart questions:

"Does this position rely heavily on the team or does it function more independently?"
"What other departments does this position work closely with or support?"
"What is the company culture like?"
"What do you love most about working here?"

An example of a question you might want to forget: "Is there room for growth?" This question is a particular pet peeve of mine because the answer is, if you're really good and the company truly values you, they will find a way to grow you. Growth doesn't always happen in the moment you believe it should, but if your boss wants you to feel supported, she will make it clear that you are on the right track to be promoted. If you ask the growth question during an interview for an entry-level position, it makes the interviewer think that you're already eyeing your next title when you don't even have your first one.

10. Do you know who your mentor is? Or who you admire? I've recommended that you find a mentor in a previous chapter, and it's possible that a potential employer could ask you who yours is. If you don't have one yet, perhaps it was a professor who took you under his wing. If you still can't think of one, that's OK. You can explain that you're

hoping to find a mentor in this next stage of your career.

11. What are your best professional attributes?

12. What is something about you that the interviewer can't learn from a resumé? Careful here; best to disclose something innocuous.

13. Did you ask for the interviewer's business card? You'll need to follow up after the interview, and it's best to never guess on spelling and title.

14. Did you THANK the interviewer(s)? Even though I am a huge fan of the written note, I've realized that the silence of not sending a timely thank-you email speaks volumes, in a bad way. Interviewers actively look out for that thank-you email. You need to send it, and you need to send it on the same day as the interview. In addition, if you met with multiple people on the team, you need to change the thank-you for each person. (If you want to go the extra mile, you can follow up with handwritten notes.) As I have stated before, you need to make sure that you thank not only the most senior person you met with, but also every person, no matter the level of that person. They all talk, you know! Picking and choosing which people to thank is a huge mistake!! In one email you can end up showing how much you really don't understand or respect the hierarchy.

Nailing the interview is one of the hardest things to do because so much of your success depends on whom you are speaking to. Besides having smart answers prepared, you need to be very aware of how your answers are being perceived. Try to consciously think about whether the interviewer seems interested in what you are saying or if you have lost her attention. If the answer is the latter, then make sure you really reboot yourself on the next topic. If you feel like you are not able to give her the answers she wants to hear, turn the tables around to her. People love talking about themselves, and asking her about her experience in the company will break the tension and take a bit of heat off you—at least for a few moments.

CHAPTER SIX

Scoring Your First Business Card

WHEN I STARTED AT *ATELIER MAGAZINE* MY SALARY WAS A WHOPPING (*S) $21,000 A YEAR. BUT I WAS LIVING AT HOME WITH MY PARENTS IN LONG ISLAND, so to me, with no bills to pay, I felt like a millionaire. Elizabeth was a warm and nurturing boss, a great second act to Dean's first. She took me under her wing immediately and I instantly felt at home. Similar to *Haute Magazine*, I was in charge of calling in accessories, maintaining the inventory and keeping the accessories closet organized.

I was ecstatic to be a genuine magazine employee and I couldn't wait to become a valuable member of the team! I didn't care if I had to pick dust bunnies out of shoes again or vacuum the closet (both of which I did), because I was finally well on my way to a career in fashion, a far cry from scrubs and rubber surgical clogs!

On the Friday of my first week at *Atelier*, it was about three in the afternoon when Elizabeth came over to my desk. "We have to return all the past-season shoes to the designers next week," she said. "So can you make sure to inventory each pair by size and sort them by designer so they can go back on Monday? Don't forget to Polaroid each pair, because nothing is worse than not having proof that the shoes were returned!"

"No problem, Elizabeth," I responded. And with that I wished her a great weekend and she left for the day.

The closet at *Atelier Magazine* was double the size of the one at *Haute*, but not nearly as nice. It had horrible wrought-iron shelving that sort of looked like army barracks. Because of the awkward length of the shelves, there was always a stray shoe that wouldn't fit, and because the vertical spacing between shelves was too high, the shoes were piled on top of each other, presumably so people didn't have to climb up to reach the higher shelves. It was a very sad sight and it clearly made it hard to maintain an orderly inventory. Not to mention, shoes were organized by color and material, and twenty pairs of black suede shoes just looked like a big black blob.

Upon Elizabeth's departure, I proceeded to go into the closet to take stock of the task at hand. I'd been in the closet before, but I hadn't yet truly absorbed its magnitude. Now considering what Elizabeth had directed me to do, my jaw fell to the floor. There were no fewer than a thousand pairs of shoes in there, and I would most definitely have to work the entire weekend to get them sorted and returned by Monday. It was the kind of moment where you think to yourself, *Wait—this is the job I dreamed of? This is why I gave up a prestigious career in medicine? To sort shoes into paper bags?*

As I started lining up large brown paper bags across the hallway, my eyes started to well up with tears. I realized the impossibility of the task at hand and wondered if Elizabeth had set this up as some crazy test of my perseverance and attitude. Labeling each shopping bag with a designer's name, I started throwing shoes into their designated bags. I had done about fifty pairs when all of a sudden I remembered that Elizabeth *also* wanted me to document *what* I was sending back. I had to unpack every pair, Polaroid them and write down their size. How could I have been so careless?! Feeling alone and totally overwhelmed, I called Cara at *Haute Magazine* for advice on how to tackle this (and perhaps for a shoulder to cry on).

"Cara? It's me, Aliza." I knew my voice was trembling and in another word I would lose it, but I continued on. "Elizabeth, my new boss, wants me to return all the old shoes in the closet by Monday. It's impossible, Cara! I swear there are over a thousand pairs in there. I don't know what to do!"

Cara was sympathetic and in disbelief. "I know Elizabeth, and I can't believe she would expect all that to be done so quickly! Are you sure? Can I come over and help you?"

"No," I replied. "You're an editor at *Haute*, you can't be helping an assistant at another magazine clean out the closet!" I assured her I wouldn't stay too late by myself (*lies*) and hung up. I felt slightly better, if only because someone else understood and felt my pain. I stayed in the closet alone until two in the morning. I think my mother called me every hour on the hour to see whether I was still alive or whether an axe murderer had broken into the office and chopped me up into little pieces. You know how whenever you're inwardly nervous about a decision you've made, you get really defensive? Every time my mom mouthed off about how she couldn't believe I'd been left alone to accomplish this ridiculous task, I yelled back about how everyone does it and you have to pay your dues (*blah, blah, blah*). But secretly, I wondered if she was right.

After sleeping about four hours, I came back to the office at seven the next morning ready to restart the hell that is sample returns. I had my system in place by then and was moving faster. But the piles of shoes on the shelves barely seemed to decrease. I worked all day with no other human in sight. I stayed there straight until three a.m. and then returned again Sunday morning and worked into the night.

By the time Monday morning rolled around I felt like I had been stomped on by a five-inch stiletto heel, but every single shoe was sorted, photographed and documented exactly the way Elizabeth wanted it.

When she showed up that morning I quickly and proudly brought her into the closet to show her the empty shoe shelves and all my countless shopping bags lined up like little soldiers. Her response? "Oh my goodness, you didn't have to do *all of it* by today!"

SAY WHAT?! Had I totally misunderstood her? Or did she realize the enormity of what she had asked for and felt embarrassed that she had made such a demand? I didn't want to question her, but I felt that I needed to understand. "Elizabeth, I thought you said that we needed to return everything by Monday?" I said.

"I meant this week," Elizabeth said. "You should have asked me to be sure."

UGH, lesson learned. **INSIDER TIP: Always clarify when the deadline is!**

Such was the life of an editorial assistant. The work was endless and the hours unyielding. Elizabeth was actually a great boss, but I basically had to come to terms with the fact that my life was no longer mine. The job required a lot of effort, and whatever it took to get the job done was what I had to do. This wasn't just at *Atelier Magazine*, it was at *Haute* too, and I'm sure countless other magazines. But I was where I wanted to be and I didn't mind one bit. I was also single back then, so I didn't really care if I worked until all hours of the night. A lot of times it was actually fun because I had the company of other fashion assistants who trudged through the trenches with me. To survive you had to make fashion your family, and so I did.

I wanted to be Elizabeth's go-to assistant, so I made sure to go above and beyond in everything she asked me to do. It worked. The more I took on, the more she let me do. In the corporate world where title is everything, Elizabeth wasn't consumed by hers versus mine. She awarded me the same access she had, and she welcomed me to interact with as many senior-level people as I could.

I was also encouraged to foster relationships with all of the public relations people at the design houses and the PR agencies. She invited me to put trend pages together and plan stories. But even though I was able to do all of that, I never once forgot that I still also needed to be the closet girl. So I wore every hat and juggled it all. The best part was that my name was actually on the masthead and I finally had my first business card! Seeing my name in print with a real title underneath it was almost better than getting my paycheck. While the whole experience still didn't feel real, the masthead and the business card were proof that I had finally broken into the fashion industry.

As I became more experienced, I started to spend a lot of time out of the office "covering the market," going on appointments and viewing collections. This, of course, enabled me to build even greater connections. I loved my job and I especially loved the perks that came with it, starting with the sample sale invitations that no one outside the fashion industry had access to. Sometimes, invitations were even limited to the accessories editors specifically. I was obsessed with sample sale shopping because it was really the only way for me to build my wardrobe at bargain-basement prices. But to get the good stuff, you had to be there really early. For example, getting to a Manolo Blahnik sample sale at five thirty a.m. for a ten a.m. opening was a regular occurrence for me. Trust me, feeling tired never crossed my mind.

Fashion editors work hard, but the upside is that they are constantly wined and dined and invited to the most glamorous parties and fashion shows. They also have a ton of access to the newest and greatest products that designers are only too happy for them to wear before anyone in the world can even buy them. When you work as a fashion editor, you can get very spoiled, very quickly. But when you're just an assistant, you can make the mistake of thinking that all those clothes and accessories in the fashion closet are normal, which then makes looking at your own closet sad and pathetic. That's pretty much where I was. I didn't have that kind of access, at least not yet, but I wanted it. The influence that came with being a fashion editor was intoxicating.

Beyond the fashion, I was constantly amazed at what I saw in the office. The talent was so impressive, the collaborative creativity even more so. The magazine was a sum of all the people who contributed to it. Working at *Atelier* made me understand why the masthead really existed; it wasn't about one person, it was about the team. At *Atelier*, I was an actual cog in the wheel of magazine production. My role was clear, and I was proud that my efforts had a real effect on those magazine pages. If I wasn't able to call in that Chanel shoe, it would never grace that magazine story. Sure, we weren't saving lives, but what we did was create aspiration for all the world to see and emulate. I was inspired and so happy.

Every morning when I walked into that massive office building with my coffee and muffin (*So caloric! Not sure what I was thinking back then*) in tow, I would stop myself for a moment to make sure that I wasn't dreaming. It didn't matter that I did a ton of physical labor—schlepping to and from with piles of shopping bags making the veins pop out of my arms. I never minded the crazy-long working hours. I embraced it all. Truth be told, it was far from glamorous, but it was my entry into a glamorous world—a world that I had only seen on the walls of my bedroom growing up.

I had come full circle. It was now my job to make a name for myself and to challenge myself to be the best I could be. I owed it to myself, but I also owed it to my parents, who had unconditionally supported my decision to quit medicine. And let's not forget Dean. Dean was the only reason I even had a job. I had to make him proud, too. I was going to do whatever it took to be successful, no matter how many hours a day or how much blood, sweat and (*hopefully not so many*) tears. I had finally started on the path I was meant to be on.

PART II

Killing It in Your Career

CHAPTER SEVEN

Going for the Promotion and the Raise

AFTER ALMOST A YEAR AND A HALF AT *ATELIER MAG-AZINE*, I HAD GREAT EXPERIENCE UNDER MY BELT. ELIZABETH LET ME TAKE ON SO MUCH THAT I FELT like I'd grown very quickly. I knew that I was doing things far beyond assistant level, and I thought that maybe that meant I should be paid beyond assistant level. Even though I had never asked for a promotion before—and really didn't know quite how to do it—I decided it was time to ask. First I broached the topic with Elizabeth. She was fully supportive of the idea, so upon her recommendation I made an appointment with Heather to discuss it.

Heather was always running to and from, and I knew she didn't have a lot of patience for small talk. So when I sat down with her, I got right to the point. "Heather, I'm so happy at *Atelier*. Elizabeth is a fantastic boss who encourages me to take on so much, but I believe that the work I do is beyond assistant level; I know that I could handle even more. Would you consider making me an associate editor?" *Silence.*

Heather stared at me with piercing eyes and then said, "Aliza, you are very lucky to be getting such vast experience, it's not a given. It is, however, your job to take on as much as you can. You are not at associate level, and I think you should keep your focus on your current position. I have a call I need to make now." Then Heather turned her attention away from me and picked up the phone.

I went back to my cubicle feeling totally defeated. I didn't know if my pitch was bad or if I had just done it too soon, so I went to consult Elizabeth. "Do you think I did something wrong?" I asked. "I hope I didn't," I continued on.

"No, I don't think you did anything wrong," Elizabeth assured me. "But Heather has her own timeline for doing things, and I'm pretty sure she thinks you need more time under your assistant belt."

I was annoyed but I guess I shouldn't have been too surprised. After all, a year and a half was not a tremendous amount of time to hold a position. It's just that I had so much responsibility, and that was confusing to me. If I was really only an assistant, then why was I doing the same level of work Elizabeth was? Heather didn't even offer to shed a tiny light at the end of the tunnel like, "You're on the right track, keep up the good work!" I started to feel like she was not going to be supportive of my growth. I loved my job, but in the back of my mind I began to worry that she was going to be the brick wall at the end of every corner I turned.

Today, nothing gives me more pleasure than being able to promote a great employee. But inevitably, there's the person who comes in at review time and starts rattling off all the things she's done that year—things that are very simply her job. You already get paid for all those things. It's called your SALARY. **INSIDER TIP: You don't get a promotion for doing your job; you get a promotion for going *above and beyond* your job.** You get a promotion by consistently managing up, which means performing on a higher level than your actual title or responsibility. From my vantage point now, people don't seem to understand that. They feel entitled just like I did back then. Maybe I was managing up, but I hadn't done it for a long enough time, and I didn't have the experience to know that. So how do you know when you deserve a promotion and how to ask for it the right way? And what do you have to do in the first place to get it?

Probably the most important thing I've learned is that in order to get the promotion of your dreams, you need to make yourself irreplaceable. That means that you are so amazing at your job that your boss would be scared to death if you left. So what you essentially want to do is make the thought of having to replace you so frightening that your boss decides it's way easier to give you a promotion (even if it means that your boss has to fight her higher-ups on your behalf) than to deal with not having you around. A great way to do this is to willingly take on various responsibilities that don't necessarily go under your job title. Meaning, if you're really doing two or three jobs in one, you are much harder to replace than someone who is doing just one. In smaller companies, or on smaller teams, this happens a lot because there just isn't the manpower to spread the work out. That can prove to be a benefit if you're smart about it. It's also easier for your boss to envision you in a more senior role if you're already playing the part. **INSIDER TIP: Act one level above the job you currently have.**

When you're ready to go in to discuss a possible promotion, you need to make sure to do several things. I've listed them below, but first and foremost you have to respect the hierarchy. Even though this conversation is most effective to have with the most senior person, you need to have it with your direct supervisor first. You must act as though you believe that your direct boss has the power and authority to promote you, even though she may not. It's about showing respect. Ultimately your boss will probably have to go to her boss to present this, but that's the way it needs to be. If you skip over your direct supervisor's head, I can assure you this promotion will not happen—and even if by some chance it does, your direct boss will resent you for it.

Take a Selfie: Are You Really Ready for a Promotion?

When you sit down in the chair across from your boss, what's your game plan? Here is what you need to ask yourself:

1. Have you gone above and beyond your job profile? Can you identify three to five things that you've accomplished that were completely innovative and unexpected? Perhaps you brought new business to the company, or came up with a successful pitch and executed it flawlessly? You have to back up any statements you make, so think these examples through.

   Next, don't just go into your boss's office and rattle off your list. Show, don't tell. Presenting on paper is more convincing than just speaking the words. It shows professionalism and dedication that you really took the time and effort to think through your own promotion. Make a presentation of your accomplishments, including as many statistics and hard facts as you can. If possible, include stats on your company's direct competition and how you've exceeded their performance within your industry.

2. Have you considered what comes next? Focus part of your pitch on what you can do for the company. For example, if you were promoted, then you could take on x, y and z, which currently aren't being managed. By attaching the idea of your promotion to the benefit of the company, you are making it easier for your boss to pitch your promotion to her boss. **INSIDER TIP: Asking for a promotion is not only about you.**

There's another way to look at this, too. Let's say that you are looking at your competition and you see that your company is falling behind. You can prepare a presentation outlining these facts in order to identify a void in your business. Your aim would be to get permission to spearhead a new project that will improve your company's rank in the industry. Identify real goals to reach. If your boss lets you pursue them and you succeed, this could be a real impetus for promotion at year-end. Regardless, you are showing that you are thinking about the company, not just yourself, and employers really like that.

3. Have you been in your current position for at least two years? I'm sorry, but that's the bogie that I've

learned along the way. In retrospect, I went for that *Atelier Magazine* promotion too soon. Now that I am an experienced manager, I don't appreciate people who work for a year and think, "OK, that's enough. Time to be bumped up!" Sorry to report that you have to pay your dues at least a little bit more than that. I know assistants who have held their exact same position and salary for at least three years. I know these days everyone believes they deserve to move up the ladder at lightning speed, but think again. Most of all, consider how much there is left to know. You don't know everything and the more you get under your belt, the better off you'll be.

Side note: The unfortunate reality is that sometimes a company doesn't recognize your value until another company tries to poach you. If you're really happy at your company and you want to grow there, you might consider interviewing elsewhere, getting a good offer and then bringing that offer back to your boss. Your hope, of course, is that your boss will recognize your worth and offer to match or at least increase your salary in an effort to keep you. But if you're going to attempt this, you need to be very prepared for the chance that your boss does not counter-offer, in which case you have no choice but to accept the other job offer. It goes without saying, but I will say it anyway, that you should never fabricate another job offer, because you could end up without any job at all. In addition, I would only recommend interviewing outside the company as a last resort.

In any industry, word travels fast and your boss might hear about your interview and not be very pleased about it. The best course of action is to always attempt growth through your own company first. But again, before you do that, make sure the time is right and you are confident that you really deserve it.

Serial job hoppers may be successful in growing their bank accounts, but if you jump from one company to another too many times, your resumé will start to look like that of a serial dater. It's not a good look, and a smart employer will not take you seriously. Remember that it takes a lot of energy and effort to train someone; if you look like you're only going to stay a year based on your track record, you won't seem worth the investment.

4. Have you done right by your boss? I know that's a weird one, as you are the one wanting the promotion, not your boss. But here's the thing: Whether you realize it or not, that is your job. **INSIDER TIP: Make your boss shine.** If you have successfully done that all year, then trust me, your boss is going to want to keep you. Making your boss shine doesn't mean ass-kissing; it means doing your job so well that you have essentially made his job that much easier while making him look great.

5. Are your clients/colleagues in love with you? Have you impressed them so many times that they actually praise you to others? If the answer is yes, then go back through your emails and include their testimonials in your presentation. Third-party credibility really weighs heavily in a

promotion. It's always better for someone else to speak on your behalf. **INSIDER TIP: Let other people promote your talents.**

6. Have you managed up? Or have you behaved and worked at least one level above your job title? To be clear, that's not to say that you should act like your boss or try to do her job. It's important that you mind your place, and you certainly don't want others to find you threatening. But the way you carry yourself in meetings and interact with people is being judged. If you act like an assistant, no one is going to be picturing you as a manager anytime soon. Again, always respect the hierarchy, but aim to perform at a higher level.

7. Are you a self-starter? Senior people don't wait to be told what to do, they just do. In order for you to be perceived as someone who can manage others, you have to take initiative and self-start projects. Are there other team members, or even interns, you can shepherd?

8. Are you a good senior mixer? Meaning, can you play and hang with the bigwigs? That's a really important skill to have. Senior people have to want to be around you. You need to fit in with that crew seamlessly. If you stick out like a sore thumb, people are not going to imagine your promotion very easily.

9. Do you present well? Are you a contributor? Do you bring new ideas to the table? Are you driving conversation or are you sitting silently? If you're uncomfortable speaking up in a large meeting or are unsure of your ideas, then you're probably not ready to take that next step.

10. Do you look the part? I honestly think that jeans and a t-shirt only work for people like Mark Zuckerberg. To me, if you want to be a senior-level person at a company, you need to be taken seriously, and the easiest way to do that is to use fashion to leverage your game. Coming to work with dirty hair, looking totally unshowered and unkempt, is not a look that screams, "Promote me!" It's a look that screams, "I don't really give a shit."

11. Do you do whatever it takes? Successful people always find a way to make the impossible happen. They know how to climb over obstacles with resourcefulness and creativity. They live by the principle that not solving the problem isn't an option.

12. Are you always "on"? Everyone has a different opinion about this, but I'm going with mine as the right one. At a certain level, a job is not just a job anymore: It is a career. If your position comes with a lot of responsibility, then your job doesn't end when the workday does, and you need to stay connected. Conversely, if you want a lot of responsibility, your boss better know that she can find you anytime, anyplace. **INSIDER TIP: Accessibility makes you indispensable.**

I truly believe that the most successful people always know what's going on with their business. That doesn't mean checking your email every hour on the hour, but it does mean checking it a few times a day, at night, on vacation, whatever. Not checking in could result in a missed opportunity—or worse, a crisis situation that could have been avoided. I don't think of checking email as work. I think of it as ensuring I'm not blindsided by anything. I am more comfortable being in the know and staying connected, and would never dream of going on vacation and completely disconnecting from the world. That idea is very uncomfortable for me. (Also, it also doesn't help that Golden Globes celebrity fittings happen in mid-December when we're all on holiday break!)

If you've honestly assessed yourself by these measurements, then you need not be afraid to go in for the kill and ask for a promotion. Even though you may be amazing at your job and go above and beyond, if you don't speak up and make your case, no one is going to come to you with the offer. Remember that there are a lot of mouths to feed at every company, so it's your job to bring your growth to your boss's attention. The worst she can say is no.

If she does say no, don't whine or complain. Even if you don't get the response you want or think you deserve, be professional. Just because you think the timing is right for a promotion doesn't mean the company does, and there could be outside reasons why a promotion is not possible right now. If you're really disappointed, you can always look for a new job elsewhere, but sometimes it makes sense to continue building your reputation at the company where you've already put in the time. It's hard to have the discipline to stay on, but if you ultimately think that there's room for growth there, it might be worth it. Of course, if you've assessed your situation honestly and you know that you're working for a boss or company who don't appreciate what you bring to the table, then it could be time to move on.

MUST DO: NEGOTIATE YOUR SALARY

When you ask for a promotion, you also need to be prepared to negotiate a salary. No one ever likes having the "money" conversation, but it's an uncomfortable reality. I get that you can just Google tips to do this, but I would be remiss if I didn't share mine. Also, isn't it just so much easier to have it all here in one place? Yeah, thought so.

1. Always know your market value. There are many online sites that post the average salaries per industry and title. Or, if you have friends at other companies in the same industry, ask them.

2. Think about what other "perks" you can ask for outside of the salary, just in case money is not an option. For example, perhaps you would consider more vacation days as a great addition to compensation. Or maybe a garment allowance? Obviously only ask for things that relate to your job.

3. Never threaten or bully your boss. Having an attitude doesn't work either. You need to be likeable and you need to prove your worth, otherwise she is not going to want to fight for you.

4. Always ask for more than you expect to receive (within reason), assuming your boss is always going to negotiate your number down. However, you always need to be mindful of the company. For example, start-up salaries are probably going to be modest compared to a long-established brand. You don't want to aim too high and knock yourself out of the game. Stay within $5,000 to $10,000 above what you really want.

5. If the offer is too low, you can politely try to prove (using market research that you have done) why you believe that

you deserve more. If you happen to know another colleague's salary in your office, do NOT mention it. Salaries are confidential and employers do not look kindly on people who discuss compensation in the office. You can, however, reference salaries at other comparable companies, but just remember that the response to that might be, "So go work there."

As they say, negotiating is an art. But your negotiating power is based so much more on the person who is listening to the pitch. You have to make sure that you have done right by your boss every step of the way, not just in the weeks leading up to your big ask. Your boss holds the key to making that promotion happen. **INSIDER TIP: Make sure your boss wants you to succeed.** I'm not discounting your talents or your high-level performance, but I'm telling you that it takes two to tango and without your boss's support, I don't care how talented you are, that promotion is not happening. Everything you do at that company should be preparing you for your promotion. You should be conscious of your efforts, your behavior and whether you're making your boss look good. Timing is everything. You need to consider the position the company is in and who else might be vying for a promotion, because you are competing from the same pool of money. Make sure you have a clear view of the landscape before you head down this road. The best time to ask for a promotion is two to three months before your company's annual review period. Don't wait for the review process because that's when everyone else (who didn't read this book) will be asking for a promotion. You want to get in there first.

CHAPTER EIGHT

Surviving People and Politics

AFTER MY FIRST-EVER ATTEMPT AT A PROMOTION TURNED OUT TO BE A TOTAL FAIL, I DECIDED THAT I HAD NO CHOICE BUT TO KEEP ON PLUGGING AWAY at work. I went back to doing my job and tried to bury my disappointment. I knew that sulking was unproductive and certainly wouldn't help the situation.

One afternoon, the team was prepping for a magazine page called "Editors' Picks," where each editor was invited to choose her favorite "item of the moment" and include a quote on why she liked it. The quote would be credited with her name and title at the magazine. Since I was an assistant, I was not usually asked to contribute to a page like this. So when Lily, our fashion director, asked me to choose my favorite shoe, I almost said, "Are you sure?!" I was both shocked and ecstatic. Maybe, despite my lack of promotion, I was finally moving up, at least in the eyes of some people on the team.

I chose my favorite Manolo Blahnik gold strappy sandal and then excitedly thought out the copy that would go on the page with my pick. I decided on "Metallics are the new black." I was proud.

A few weeks later, when the page was being routed around the department for fact-checking, I was summoned to Heather's desk. She was FURIOUS, and I was so confused and scared because I had no idea what I'd done. She proceeded to accuse me of promoting myself and changing my job title. HUH?? I was floored. She showed me the Editors' Picks page and there was my shoe selection, complete with my little quote, my name and my title of assistant accessories editor. I still didn't get it. What was wrong?

"Heather, I'm sorry, I don't see what is wrong with the page," I said innocently.

"Aliza, read the title to me," she said sternly.

"It says 'assistant accessories editor,'" I read cautiously.

"Well, that is NOT your title! How dare you try to promote yourself when I was VERY clear that you were NOT GETTING A PROMOTION!!"

I was stunned. *REALLY?!* I couldn't believe my ears.

"Heather, I would never, ever promote myself. I totally respect your decision," I countered. "It's just that assistant accessories editor *is* my title. It's what's written on my business card."

"Well, maybe you printed your own business card! For all I know, you're trying to take my job or even take over this whole magazine!" screamed Heather.

To be clear, I was twenty-three years old! I could not even comprehend this conversation. It was so unfair and so irrational!! But sometimes when I'm in shock, I have this weird out-of-body experience where I get numb to a situation and have no fear. I calmly and respectfully responded,

"Heather, I would never dream of being as qualified as you are. As far as the title, I am happy to call human resources with you right now so they can confirm that my title is, in fact, assistant accessories editor. I think this is simply a miscommunication and I am so sorry that you're so upset." But she didn't want to hear it. With a wave and a strong huff, she dismissed me.

From that day on, I knew something very clearly about fashion: The higher up you are, the harder your ego can fall. Insecurity is the root of all evil, and there are just some people you can't win with.

Upon leaving Heather's desk I quickly ran to the bathroom. As I passed other desks, I tried to not look in anyone's direction out of fear that I would burst into tears. *How could this be happening? What did I do to make Heather hate me so much?* In the bathroom I went into a stall and tried to reason with myself. *Could I have acted differently? Wait. That was my title, right?* I started to panic that I had imagined it. I quickly left the bathroom and went back to my desk as inconspicuously as possible. When I sat down, I quietly opened my drawer and pulled out a business card. There it was in bold black type: assistant accessories editor. Heather was completely out of her mind, but it didn't matter; she was the boss and her opinion was the only opinion. I decided in that moment that I had to be on my best behavior. Not that I wasn't prior to this incident, but it was time to go deeply under the radar.

As the next few weeks passed by, I made sure to just do my job and keep to myself. When I was in Heather's presence, I played the role of the serious underling, rather than showing my normal jubilant personality. I had to show her that I knew my place and that I didn't think I was this high-flying editor. I also made sure to steer clear of her whenever possible.

One day, Heather's assistant came by my desk to tell me that Heather needed to give a gift to the magazine's publisher but that she didn't actually want to buy it; she'd rather be gifted something from a designer, which she could then re-gift to the publisher. She wanted an evening clutch of sorts, and apparently it was my job to get it. I wasn't happy about the task—first of all, because I thought it was really tacky that she couldn't just buy a gift with her kind of salary, and second, because I felt uneasy about doing her dirty work. But alas, I had no choice. On the bright side, maybe if I did the task well she might have a better opinion of me!

I called around to several designers to see if they were willing to graciously give Heather a sample. Sure enough, Bottega Veneta was willing to donate one of their signature woven bags. I nailed that task in three phone calls and I was super excited to show Heather how fast I'd done it. I proudly went to see her with the two woven satin clutches I was given as options. She was meant to choose the color she preferred and then I would just return the other one back to the designer. Well, I didn't get that far.

"Woven?! You got me woven?! I gave her a woven bag LAST YEAR!" Heather yelled.

"I'm so sorry, Heather, I had no idea. I can return them and get you other options," I said.

"I told Jeremy to tell you that," Heather snapped. Jeremy, Heather's assistant, promptly appeared.

"Aliza, didn't you see that email?" Jeremy asked.

"No? I'm sorry I don't recall ever seeing an email specifying the bag style," I countered.

"Well, I sent it," Jeremy curtly replied. I was speechless. I had failed Heather again.

I went back to my desk feeling nauseated. How could I have done this? I quickly checked my email inbox and found no email from Jeremy. Then I checked the email's trash. Nothing. I walked back over to Jeremy's desk. "Jeremy, I'm certain that I don't have an email from you," I stated.

"I know. I forgot to send it," he said with a smirk, and then he got up and walked away. I was in utter shock.

At that moment my eyes welled with tears. Of course, I would rather die than show Jeremy that they'd gotten to me, but boy, had they ever. I realized that when Jeremy was faced with saving himself or throwing me under the bus, he chose to see me with tire marks.

But I knew that was it, the last straw. I had held on for long enough and I knew that no matter how hard I worked, I would never get anywhere with Heather. It was time to look for a new job. It was a shame though, because Heather aside, I loved working at *Atelier*. Not only had I made a great group of friends, I was generally doing well in my position, at least as far as Elizabeth was concerned. But Heather was the roadblock, and I realized that there was nothing I could do to change her perception of me.

MUST DO: KNOW THE PLAYERS

If I had been more experienced, I might have handled Heather differently. In retrospect, I could have stroked her ego more by being more reserved around her from the beginning. She wanted me to be intimidated. In Heather's mind, I had dues to pay. I also never contemplated that some people would not want me to succeed, especially because Elizabeth was so totally support-ive of me. It's called office politics, kids, and it's a big, fat game.

While it's essential for you to have a strong sense of self, you have to know whom you're dealing with. If you're in the sand-box, you need to know which kid is going to throw the sand.

The bad players in the game of office politics can very easily be summed up by many of the iconic characters I grew up with. These personalities exist on every team, in every industry, all over the world. Get to know your colleagues before it's too late.

1. **Maggie Simpson:** The quintessential baby. This is the per-son in your office who is constantly complaining, helpless and oversensitive. Best to never joke or test out your sarcas-tic humor with Maggie. She'll go crying to Mommy, a.k.a. your boss.

2. **Mr. T:** The super-aggressive coworker who rules by bullying. Mr. T wants you to be intimidated, so if you want to have a peaceful office existence, you might consider lying low when you're in his presence.

3. **She-Ra, Princess of Power:** There's only "I" in this person's alphabet. If you're paired on She-Ra's team, just know that she'll try to take all the credit for whatever the collective team does. Cover yourself early with your boss by putting everything in writing. A responsibility chart will also make it clear so your boss knows who is handling what.

4. **Batman:** The person who changes who he is depending on whom he's with. He's the guy who will say yes to your face and then turn around and tell someone else that he said no. Watch your back and ask for things in writing.

5. **The Joker:** The giant-mouthed person who thinks yelling is an acceptable form of communication. Every office has a

Joker. When dealing with him it's best not to give in to the drama and remain calm and even-keeled. Do not lower your professional standards to match his.

6. **Mr. Potato Head:** Giant head. Giant ego. There's only one opinion that matters and you can guess whose that is. With Mr. Potato Head it's best to not openly compete for the spotlight. If you don't strike him as a threat, you'll be much better off.

7. **Malibu Barbie:** The person who thinks work is what other people do. You don't want to work with Barbie, because she's not going to lift a finger. If you find her on your team, make sure your job responsibilities are clearly defined so that when she doesn't do her part, you don't get blamed for it.

8. **Ken:** The person who gets by simply because of good looks. Ahh, good old Ken, he'll be promoted and get a hefty title because he "looks the part" and plays a good game. These types are lucky and they totally get by for superficial reasons. It's not fair, but nothing ever is. The rest of us just have to have work harder. Sorry.

9. **Mr. Spacely:** The all "fluff" boss who has a big title and doesn't actually do ANYTHING. Mr. Spacely is probably the most annoying boss to have, because you know the truth about him, but sadly his peers do not. We all work for Mr. Spacely at one point or another and it's important to make sure that the "powers that be" know your worth and what you do. That can be accomplished by making sure any report you generate ends with the strategic last comment: "If anyone has any questions or comments, please contact [your name]."

10. **Gargamel:** The person who steals other people's ideas and serves them up as his own. Gargamel is one of the most

unlikeable personalities there are because his intentions are bad. To combat him, put every idea you have in writing and make sure to cc your boss and the rest of the country while you're at it.

11. **Cruella de Vil:** The person whose primary goal is to start and spread gossip about coworkers in order to advance. Cruella is the worst offender, and the only way to defend yourself against her is to a) stay away from her and b) don't give her any reason to talk about you. Mind your reputation and P.S., don't gossip about her either!

12. **Oscar the Grouch:** The perma-negative person who thinks the world (or at least the company) is coming to an end daily. You can't let Oscar get you down. He will try to bring you into his dark and stormy world, and you will start to question why you work at that company at all. But don't let him get into your head. His negativity should be his own problem—not yours.

13. **Dopey Smurf:** This person is so clueless it's a wonder he knows how to get dressed in the morning. Dopey probably got the job because his mom is a socialite or his dad owns a baseball team. You know the type. He's usually harmless. Just ignore him and be happy that you have so many more brain cells than he does.

The skills you hone are only half of the recipe for success. You need much more than talent to survive people and office politics. To really succeed, you also need to be a master of human nature. Bottom line: If you can't learn how to work with all different types of people, it really doesn't matter how GOOD you are at what you do.

So my secret job hunt began. The first job I heard about was an accessories editor position open at *Muse*. *Muse* wasn't a magazine that I would automatically gravitate toward, but the thought of being an actual editor was tempting. I had a PR friend reach out on my behalf to see if the fashion director was interested in meeting with me. I was thrilled to hear that she was. I was even more excited when I learned that before I went in to meet with her, she wanted me to put together inspiration boards for an upcoming story they were planning to shoot. I love a good creative project and I was hopeful that my eye for fashion would stand out.

When you work at a magazine, every story is visually planned out before any actual product is called in. This is called "making a board." Back in the day, the board was usually made from good old cork, and the editor could pin what she visualized for the story. But it was a bit tedious. You see, when photographers shot runway shows, their film was converted into these things called "slides." Magazines would have boxes upon boxes of slides, each box reflecting a different designer's collection. When making a board, you would take the appropriate slides and, using a slide machine, convert them into actual photographs that you could then pin to your board.

Because fashion editors are generally very specific, they each had their own way that they liked the boards done, and even had preferences about how the photograph was to be made from the slide. For most fashion editors, it was essential to see the model's head in the photograph, because it helped remind them who wore the look on the runway (with the idea that the best models got the best looks). But the machine that converted the slides was not an easy device to manage, and oftentimes you would end up chopping off a bit of the model's head by accident. If that happened, you had to start over. If you accidentally pinned a model's picture with the head slightly cropped, you were pretty much a dead man. It's just the way it was.

I knew that I would have to do this perfectly and probably over and over again for my *Muse* board, so I decided to borrow a photographer friend's machine so I could do the work at home and really focus. In many cases I had to remake a photo several times just to get the top of the head correct. For accessories shots I used my tiny nail scissors to make sure they were cut out perfectly. You know when you work on something and you know, unquestionably, that you did a great job? I knew I had nailed this. I was so excited to share my work with the fashion director; the interview couldn't come soon enough.

On the day of the interview, I carried my boards (I had made two) like newborn babies in a large handbag, making sure not to bend or crinkle the pictures in any way. I arrived at the *Muse* offices fifteen minutes early. Better you wait for them than the other way around. My interview was supposed to be at noon. Remember, back then there were no smartphones to play with, so while I waited for the fashion director to summon me from the lobby, I just sat there, staring at my red nails. At around 12:20 p.m., I glanced at my watch and couldn't believe how late it was. I didn't have the luxury of spending so much time out of my real office, and I was starting to get nervous that someone back at *Atelier* would begin to wonder where I was. Sometimes I am convinced that people make you wait on purpose to show you "look how busy and important I am!" By 12:45 p.m., I was starting to get the feeling that the fashion director was one of those people.

At exactly 1:00 p.m., her assistant came to the lobby and summoned me to follow her. Great, I had wasted an hour and fifteen minutes of my life that I would never get back. The assistant was a quiet girl who looked very nervous and fidgety.

"Busy day?" I asked.

The assistant looked at me blankly and said, "No." *Fabulous. This was going to be fun.* (*S)

AssistantX brought me into yet another room that didn't look like an office. The fashion director was nowhere in sight. "Am I to wait here?" I asked. "Yes, she will be in shortly," she replied. *More waiting? Was this woman serious?* Clearly my time meant nothing to her, and more importantly, she was very keen to show me how important and busy she was.

At 1:15 p.m., the fashion director came in. She must have been five ten barefoot and then with heels, add another four inches. Her brown pin-straight hair hung shoulder length, and her lips looked like they rarely moved to form a smile. She hadn't even opened her mouth but she was already scaring me.

"Hi, Alessandra, it's a pleasure to meet you," I said in a friendly tone as I outstretched my arm to shake her hand.

"Do you have your boards to show me?" she replied dryly, her piercing green eyes burning a hole through mine. *Gulp.*

I reached down to carefully pull the boards out of my handbag and saw her looking at me as if to say, "Why are you taking so long?" She had made me wait an hour and fifteen minutes, and she was already rushing me in the first two minutes of our meeting. My excitement to present the boards was quickly turning to dread. I pulled the boards out and put them on the table for her review. As I started to explain my vision for the storyboards, she quickly interrupted me.

"You cropped some models' heads. That's really not acceptable here."

WHAAAAAAT?! My models' heads were perfect. "I'm sorry, Alessandra, I really don't see what you are referring to. Do you mind showing me the example?" I asked respectfully.

"Are you saying that I'm seeing things that aren't there?" she exclaimed.

"No, not at all. I was just wondering where you see a cropped head, because to my eye they are all perfectly accounted for," I responded carefully.

"Well, I'm not going to point it out. If you can't see it, then obviously you're not right for the position," she said.

And just like that, my interview was over. I was stunned into silence. Before I could even say, "Thank you for taking the time to meet with me," she had excused herself. (Yes, even in my most blown-off state, I still tried to utilize my manners.) AssistantX came in with a knowing look, as if she had seen this many times before.

"Is she always this tough?" I asked her.

She looked at me with blank eyes and said, "I don't know what you're talking about." In the distance I saw Alessandra staring at us.

I headed back to my office completely flabbergasted. For starters, it was so incredibly late. I had no idea what was waiting for me when I returned. Second, OMFG what a nightmare!! Forget about all the hard work and thought I had put into those boards; I could never work for a person like that. How could there be yet another Heather? I couldn't believe it and it made me really sad. Was this going to be the case at every magazine? I sincerely hoped not. I needed to find another boss like Elizabeth or Dean so desperately!

When I got back to my office, it was quiet and business as usual. Thankfully, my whereabouts were not questioned. When I sat back down at my computer, my first thought was about the thank-you note, but I decided to wait until I got home so I could better think about what on earth I was going to say. Thank you for making me wait forever? Thank you for being insane? I couldn't believe I had to thank that awful person for anything. But I decided that I wasn't going to compromise my standards because hers were in the gutter. Later that night I drafted the below:

From: Aliza Bernfeld
To: Alessandra Rossi
Subject: Thank you

Dear Alessandra,
   Thank you so much for taking the time to meet with me today. I really enjoyed putting those boards together for your consideration and I feel that my vision for your shoots reflected the *Muse* girl's style. I'm sorry that you took issue with the way my models' heads were cropped; I really did try to crop them as immaculately as possible. I hope that you will consider the fashion point of view exemplified in my product choices, as surely that is what makes a great fashion editor, like yourself.
   Sincerely,
   Aliza Bernfeld

PUKE. BULLSHIT. BLAH. But you know what? I felt good about it. A little ass-kissing might just make her reconsider me and make me an offer that I couldn't WAIT TO REFUSE.

Meeting people like Alessandra always makes for a good eye-opener. There are people out there who care only about themselves, their status and their position. Insecurity, unfortunately, runs rampant in every industry. Oftentimes it's because people have failed up. On one hand, your goal on an interview is to impress and to share why you would be an asset to the company. On the other hand, you might be faced with someone like Alessandra, who can't bear the thought of having someone with fresh talent on her team. That's why, as much as an interview is an employer's opportunity to see if she wants you, it's also equally as important for you to consider if you actually want to work for her. I could never work for someone who didn't want me to be confident or talented. Finding that out early was a blessing in disguise. **INSIDER TIP: You should never dumb yourself down to land a job.** If you do so, you will never be maximizing your potential.

A few weeks later, I bumped into a junior editor at *Muse* who had resigned because apparently someone had been poking holes in the heads of his boards while he was away from his desk. It was an office mystery, and they couldn't figure out who would do such a crazy thing! Funny, I knew exactly who. We chatted for a few minutes and then I said, "Did you ever find out who poked all those holes in your board?"

"I was never able to actually prove who did it, but I have a sneaky suspicion that it was Alessandra," he said.

Ah-ha! "Why would she want to sabotage you?!" I questioned.

"Because she doesn't like when other people excel, and I was doing really well there. The editor in chief was coming to me instead of her, because I, unlike her, actually did the work and had the answers." Yes, this all made sense. I wasn't crazy. The situation was exactly like I had imagined.

That junior editor should have never quit. He should have marched himself into the editor in chief's office and laid it all on the line. I have a real problem with people being pushed around unfairly, and since tho junior editor seemed to have the editor in chief's ear, it probably would have been a successful meeting for him. But some people can't deal with confrontation and would rather just remove themselves from the situation. Something I've learned though, office drama is pretty much a given. No matter the industry, there will always be an Alessandra or an Alessandro waiting in the wings. If you're going to let people like that stand in your way, you're not giving yourself a chance to succeed. **INSIDER TIP: Develop a thick skin.**

The goal should always be to learn how to work around the troublemakers. Sometimes though, you have no choice but to out bad behavior. But before you go around accusing someone of anything, you need to make sure you have all the facts. There's risk associated with tattling, so your investigative work needs to be at Olivia Pope levels. Outing a rat could backfire too, but at least you tried. The junior editor gave up a great job even though the most important person there, the editor in chief, valued him. He should have fought for himself, because if you don't fight for yourself, no one else will.

Take a Selfie: Are You Working for Regina George?

To be clear, this is not just about women. Just look at Jeremy from *Atelier*. I've seen many a man exemplify the same kind of behavior, but *Mean Girls* was such a great movie, wasn't it?

How do you know if you have a boss who at first appears professional, but is really out to squash you?

1. She tells you not to speak unless spoken to—under the guise of "protecting you" from sharks in the meeting. Then after the meeting, she questions why you were so quiet.

2. She leaves out key pieces of information that you need to do the project you've been handed. For example, she asks you to make a list of the top TV shows and then neglects to tell you, "But only those starring teenagers." Then when you hand in your list she says, "Why are there forty-year-olds on here?"

3. She never gives you credit for your ideas and presents them as her own. This one is tricky, as it is often your job to generate ideas for your boss. But at the same time, letting the light shine on you once in a while is a gracious thing to do.

4. She never lets you sit in on important meetings that your peers are invited to and asks that you not email executives directly.

5. She always finds fault with the work you do, when you know you've done exactly what she asked for.

6. She asks you to do menial tasks that you know don't need to be done. For example, separating paper clips by color. Yes, that happens.
7. She asks you for the password to your email and voicemail, just in case she needs it if you're out sick. (Spy!!!)
8. She yells at you for ridiculous things like ordering the wrong rubber bands. She wanted skinny ones!! Not thick ones!!!!
9. She gets mad at you when you call in sick, as if you can control that.
10. She accuses you of wanting her job.

Every office and every industry has politics, and no matter what business you are in, there are always going to be people who are trying to get ahead using questionable tactics. Heather and Alessandra had used the same kind of irrational sabotage to trip me up. With Heather, it was how she took fault with my title (and probably my confidence), and with Alessandra, it was with my fictitious cropped model heads. But with Jeremy, he was just about saving himself, making me take the fall for a mistake he made. But get ready, because there's another type of office player, and this one might be the scariest of them all.

If you're a normal, sane person, it's hard sometimes to comprehend how someone else isn't. I always tend to believe that people are just like me, so I rarely find myself looking for surefire clues to their certifiable insanity. But over the years, I've heard some crazy stories—starring the kind of people who are scary precisely because their craziness is not immediately obvious. In fact, they're so good at their deceptive brand of crazy that sometimes you start to think it's *you*, not them. We might call these people the "Talented Mr. Ripley" types.

At a very reputable magazine, a guy named Charles was hired to head up advertising sales. He was handsome, tall and dapper and played the creative-fashion-type role very well. When he entered a room, people noticed. Charles was also really friendly and collaborative, a perfect counterbalance to his seeming perfection, which would have been enough for anyone to resent him.

Zoe was a colleague of Charles's and an editor at the same magazine. In the magazine business, editorial and advertising are a bit like church and state. Zoe and Charles of course worked together, but not on a regular basis. However, their limited interaction was very pleasant, and Zoe and the team found Charles very likeable.

Until one day, when Charles left Zoe this voicemail: "Zoe, I need to talk to you about Amanda. There's a problem."

Wow, Zoe thought. *Amanda?* Amanda had been on her team for almost three years and everyone loved working with her. In fact, Charles was the first person to ever raise an issue about her. Zoe was particularly upset to hear this as Amanda was being groomed to grow at the company.

Zoe called him back. "Hi, Charles, it's Zoe, what happened with Amanda?"

"Zoe, I hate to be the one to tell you this, but she was really rude to Paul. She basically blew his head off when he didn't have the advertising analysis report she needed for her editorial meeting."

"Really?!" Zoe said. "That just sounds so out of character for Amanda. But I will speak to her immediately."

Zoe hung up the phone in disbelief. It just seemed so hard to believe, but Charles had no reason to lie. Zoe called Amanda into her office and asked her to sit down.

"Amanda, what happened with Paul?" Zoe asked.

"Paul? Nothing," she said.

"Was he able to get you the report you needed for the meeting?" Zoe prompted her.

"No," she said. "But it was really last-minute and he just couldn't pull it together in time."

Zoe wasn't getting anywhere but she didn't want to lead the witness. "Is there any reason you can think of for Paul to be upset with you?" Zoe asked.

"No?" Amanda replied with a bit of wonder.

Zoe thanked Amanda and excused her, asking her to close the door as she walked out so she could call Paul herself.

"Paul, it's Zoe. I just wanted to understand what happened between you and Amanda."

Paul responded, "I'm not sure what you're talking about."

"You're not angry at Amanda? She wasn't rude to you?" Zoe asked with disbelief.

"Amanda? No, we get along great," Paul replied. *Right.* That's what Zoe thought—so what the hell was Charles talking about??

Zoe told Paul what Charles had told her and he couldn't believe his ears. Zoe was beside herself. *Charles lied?! Deliberately, to start trouble? What kind of person not starring in a Lifetime movie would do such a thing?* In that moment Zoe realized that she was not dealing with a normal person. She decided that she needed to call Charles out on his lie.

"Hi, Charles, I wanted to update you on my conversation with Amanda and Paul," Zoe said when she called Charles again.

"You called Paul?!" Charles exclaimed incredulously.

"Well, yes, I mean, you made it sound like Paul was really, really upset, so of course I needed to check in with him," Zoe responded. "Funny thing though (*S), Paul didn't know what I was talking about."

"Well, that's crazy," Charles retorted. "He was very put off by it."

"No, actually he has no idea what you're talking about," Zoe countered. "So the question is where on earth did you get this story from?" Zoe asked.

That's when Charles lost it and started screaming and going on and on about how dare Zoe accuse him of lying, blah, blah, blah. Zoe just sat on the phone in silence and waited for Charles to be finished. When he was, or at least stopped to take a breath, Zoe very calmly said, "I think we should agree to disagree on what happened. I have to go into a meeting now. Bye."

From that day on, Zoe vowed to never speak to Charles on the phone again. She also advised everyone on her team to do the same. Charles was a liar and a troublemaker and could not be trusted. So every time he called one of them, they would just let it go to voicemail, then email him back saying, "I got your voicemail. I'm out on an appointment. What's up?" Zoe would then print every email and put it into a "Charles" folder. It's pretty unreal that Zoe had to go to these extremes to deal with him, but Charles was dangerous. The paper trail was the only solution.

One day Aubrey, a PR girl from a well-known agency that reps an eyewear brand, called Zoe to tell her that the "eyewear she wanted for her shoot" was ready to be picked up. Zoe was confused. *What eyewear and what shoot?* So she casually mentioned to Aubrey that she didn't know what she was referring to. Aubrey responded, "You know, the styles Charles called in."

Whaaaaat?! thought Zoe in a panic. Charles didn't speak to PR agencies; he was on the business side. But besides that, Charles was infringing on relationships that had taken Zoe years to build. If Charles had needed eyewear for any reason, the normal protocol would have been to ask Zoe to call them in for him. Zoe asked Aubrey to send her any email correspondence between her and Charles. After reading the thread, it was clear that Charles had completely overstepped his boundaries—even going as far to say that Zoe wanted him to reach out.

Zoe had never been faced with a work situation like this before. Either Charles wanted her job or he wanted to get her fired for not doing her own job. Bottom line: This needed to be addressed. So Zoe emailed Charles to ask why he had called in the product himself, without speaking to her, and what this alleged shoot was all about:

From: Zoe Fitzpatrick
To: Charles Williams
Subject: Eyewear shoot?

Dear Charles,
    I got a phone call today from Aubrey, who told me that the eyewear you requested on my behalf was ready to picked up for my photo shoot. As I know nothing about this request, can you explain?

From: Charles Williams
To: Zoe Fitzpatrick
Subject: Re: Eyewear shoot?

Dear Zoe,
   You have it all wrong. I was at dinner with
Aubrey because you know we are old friends
and I happened to mention a shoot that's
coming up and she suggested that she send
over the eyewear. It was totally her idea and
it was no big deal!
   Charles

The thing was, Zoe had Charles's email, which clearly said, "Zoe asked me to call in" and "for her photo shoot." There had been so many half-truths and full-on lies in the past few months that Zoe couldn't believe how stupid Charles was to negate Aubrey's statements on email. Apparently Charles had guessed that Zoe wouldn't bother to check. Sorry, Charlie.

Zoe called human resources to set up an appointment to discuss the situation and asked that they invite Charles to join. The "Charles" file had gotten really big at this point, one inch big. The papers were hidden in Zoe's handbag so Charles had no idea what was in store for him.

Zoe's strategy in confrontational meetings was always to remain calm and professional, because nothing makes people more upset than someone they can't anger. So Zoe began the meeting by simply saying that she wanted to state for the record the differences between her job and Charles's so that they could better establish (or reestablish) Zoe's responsibilities versus his. Then Zoe asked Charles outright why he contacted Aubrey, even though Zoe already knew what Charles's excuse was.

Charles immediately went on the defense and started ranting in anger. He started off with the lie that he already told Zoe about his dinner with Aubrey, etc. etc., and WHY was she asking him something that she already knew the answer to *blah, blah, blah*. Well, she was asking so that Charles could lie right in front of human resources.

That's when Zoe lifted her very large and very heavy handbag off the floor and busted out all the printed emails. Then she calmly looked at Charles and said, "Shall we go through this pile to find your email to Aubrey? Actually, I think I have it right here at the top." There was nothing Charles could say about anything that Zoe didn't have the proof to negate. It was time to go in for the killer question. "Charles, I'm starting to get the sense that you want my job. Would you like to have my job?" Zoe demanded.

Then Charles blurted out, "If I wanted your job, I could have it! I would do it better than you and I have contacts that would do amazing things for this magazine." Zoe didn't have to say anything more because that's when human resources took over. There were boundaries to each position—and no, Charles couldn't just contact his "PR agency friend" to call in accessories for a fake shoot, just as Zoe couldn't just call a company and try to sell them ad pages.

Zoe's mission was accomplished. She had exposed Charles's psychotic side and she felt so much better now that she was no longer the only person who knew about it. In life, people make their own beds, and Charles had made his. Don't feel bad for Charles, though; the Talented Mr. Ripley always moves on and finds other prey. And so he failed up, this time by moving to a different company where no one knew he was a sociopath...yet.

MUST DO: LEARN TO WORK WITH THE TALENTED MR. RIPLEY

1. Cover your bum. This type of coworker is bound to try to find a way to point the finger at you at some point. Make sure you have your bases covered and your record is squeaky clean. You don't want to give him anything to use against you.
2. Maintain decorum. As painful as it is, bite your tongue and keep your cool. Be respectful and professional at all times, even when you're being pushed to lose it. Remember, he wants you to lose it.
3. As much as possible make sure all communication you have with this person is in writing. I mean everything. Operate as if the phone does not exist.
4. Keep a record. If push ever came to shove, your memory will fail you; that's why it's imperative that you save any examples of bad behavior. If it gets really out of control, your case will build itself. Then you can present a really professional and legitimate list of examples instead of just whining about someone. If you show up with ten pages written about your coworker, no one is going to think you made it all up.
5. Try to limit dealings alone with this person as much as possible. In meetings, make sure that there are witnesses to whatever strategy is being discussed.
6. If it gets to a boiling point, do discuss the situation with your boss or human resources department. Sometimes it is

hard to handle these things alone. Before you do so though, make sure you have all your ducks in a row.

7. Don't vent! The worst thing you can do is start mouthing off about your colleague to other people, internal or external. If you feel you must, do so with someone far removed from your industry. No one keeps a secret!! The expression "I'm just telling *you* this" has been told to countless people.

8. Remember that every job you have follows you to the next one. So even though you want to completely obliterate your relationship with the Talented Mr. Ripley, it's really not smart to. People move around a lot within industries and it's essential that you don't burn bridges. People come out of the woodwork, and you really don't want to put yourself in a situation where you have to work with or for that same person again, in a different capacity—and you can't because he hates you.

In any business, politics and personalities are very tricky. Sometimes politics can ruin a perfectly good job experience, so learning to navigate the waters is one of the most important skills you can learn. You always need to remember your worth and maintain your standards of professionalism, no matter what. There will always be difficult people and there will always be insecure people, but at the end of the day you can't sacrifice yourself or your dreams because you're scared to face these people head-on. Don't ever let anyone squash your spirit. Confidence is a blessing. Work your rock star attitude and shine on, but always respect the hierarchy. Give every situation 200 percent so that if it doesn't work out, you know you tried. But P.S., sometimes you'll realize that you're actually too good for a job and if they can't see that, the right answer is to move on.

CHAPTER NINE

Shifting Gears and Getting Ahead

ONCE I KNEW THAT MY DAYS AT *ATELIER* WERE NUM-
BERED AND THE POSITION AT *MUSE* WAS NOT GOING
TO WORK OUT, I TRIED TO INTERVIEW ELSEWHERE.
It's sad when you have to pull the plug on what you thought
would be your dream job—but it's better to be honest with
yourself and move on than hang around and wait for the shit
to really hit the fan. I managed to secure other interviews,
but they led nowhere. It seemed that every editor at every
magazine that I was interested in had been in his or her role
for at least ten years with no sign of ever leaving. There was
no room for growth. I couldn't wait years to be an editor.

Was I being impatient? I guess. Sure, I could have taken
another assistant position and really built up my experience. But something made me feel that was the wrong
move for me. My experience at *Atelier* had been so comprehensive that I didn't want to be bored somewhere else. I felt
like I had been there, done that. I was over it. Whether I was
right or wrong I'll never know, but I believed it was time to

broaden my horizons. I needed something new—a different kind of challenge.

In any business, you need to think of your industry like an onion: What are the layers that surround it? What's the circle that surrounds your immediate circle? In my immediate circle there were editors, stylists, copy editors, feature writers, etc. What surrounded that circle were all the people who helped us do our jobs: designers and the publicists who represent them. Since you can't live in a bubble, it's important to always see what's in arm's reach and to be able to visualize yourself in another role. That is what I had done when I was on the "sell side" at *DC Moment*; I looked just beyond the ad sales team to the people who worked in editorial. **INSIDER TIP: Don't just learn your job, learn everyone else's.**

With that in mind, I started to think about the PR people I spoke to all day long while calling in the accessories I needed for the shoots we did at *Atelier*. After all, just by doing my job, I'd come to know how those PR people did theirs. More importantly, I knew the difference between the people who were good at their jobs and those who were not. In any client relationship, you know whom you want to work with and whom you don't. It was the perfect crash course for how to become a good PR person.

I started calling around to editors I knew at different magazines to see if they had heard of any open positions in PR. I felt this was a much better, more top-secret way to gather information on open positions without putting myself out there too much. After all, who better to know who was hiring in PR than the editors who spoke to PR people all day? It was a great way to investigate my options without actually calling prospective companies directly. **INSIDER TIP: Leverage your existing network to job hunt.** People who call companies directly are inevitably at a disadvantage. There's a big difference between needing a job and casually seeing what's out there. I wanted to have the upper hand.

I heard that a junior PR position had become available at DKNY. I had grown up with DKNY—in fact, I grew up one town over from where Donna Karan herself had been raised. It was familiar to me. I liked Donna Karan as a designer and I was interested in trying my hand at public relations. But I wasn't going to call DKNY myself. Instead I asked an editor friend at another magazine to recommend me, while pretending, of course, that I had no idea that she was going out on such a limb for me. *Wink.* **INSIDER TIP: Third-party credibility is always more powerful than anything you can ever say on your own behalf.**

When you think about it, what else did I have in my favor except a good recommendation? It's not like I had practical PR experience. I had to highlight something about myself that was unique and superior to the other potential candidates who did have that direct experience.

One morning my phone rang at *Atelier Magazine*. "Hi, this is Amy from DKNY. Is this Aliza?"

"Yes, this is she," I said. Here's where I acted like I had no idea that Amy would be calling about a position. My strategy was to play it cool.

"We have an open position for someone to work on accessories PR and EditorX gave me your name. Is this something you would be interested in talking about?" *Duh.*

"Oh, that's so nice of EditorX to think of me. I definitely want to hear more about the position," I said. A few days later I went in to interview and even surprised myself with how much I knew about PR based on how much I knew about editorial. My former job taught me my next job; they were two sides of the same coin. That's why it's always so important to learn the jobs of the people you work with. I had essentially trained myself in public relations without any actual PR experience.

Shortly thereafter, Amy called to offer me the position. I asked for the offer in writing. I was quite demanding for having had little professional experience, but I wanted to make sure that we had a clear understanding. I didn't want to resign from *Atelier* unless I was positive that I had another job! Getting that letter was one of my proudest moments. It signified the beginning of my career in public relations.

I started at DKNY on August 17, in the dead of the summer. The office was on 40th Street right off the infamous 7th Avenue, in the heart of the garment center. The whole building belonged to DKNY, and the PR office commanded the twelfth floor, right off of the showroom. I was so excited to embark on this new journey, but when I got there I couldn't believe how similar my new job was to the position I had at *Atelier.*

Even though I was now in public relations (with another cherished business card to prove it), I was still doing the same type of work that I'd done at *Atelier Magazine* and *Haute Magazine* before that. My title was now assistant accessories PR coordinator (trust me, I made sure to check that business card more than twice!), which put me right back in the closet, keeping tabs on hundreds of bags and shoes.

A lot of people might see what I did as a lateral move. In fact, these days I interview people all the time who come in concerned about a potential position being too lateral to their last one, saying that if they're going to take a new job, they want to make more money and have more responsibility. While that may be valid, sometimes you have to look at opportunities in a different way. Sometimes you can't just look at the *job* as the key to your career growth. You have to consider your new company, your new boss and your new work environment, too. It's not a lateral move if you're going from a boss you never learned anything from to a new boss who will ultimately serve as your career mentor. It's also not a lateral move if you're going from an obscure company to a major global brand. It's not only about your new title, salary and day-to-day schedule. **INSIDER TIP: Judge a job on its future potential. A seemingly lateral move could ultimately prove to be the opportunity of a lifetime.**

I knew the public relations industry would offer me more career options than staying in magazine editorial would. Sure, the tasks were often similar, and menial at that, but I kept constantly telling myself that one day those tasks would be long behind me. I decided to keep my eye on the present and forget about the future. I relished not having a goal. After all, how did my longtime goal of becoming a doctor help me? The organic process of letting choices become clear as they are meant to seemed like a much better idea. Quitting medicine made me reignite my love for fashion magazines; learning the magazine industry allowed me to learn the PR industry. I never planned to be a publicist; it's just where the path led me. **INSIDER TIP: Forget the long-term career goal. Nail what is in front of you and your next step will become crystal clear.** To me, it's way more important to get your foot in a door that shows promise and give 200 percent to whatever that is. If you succeed and make an impression, another door is bound to open.

Public relations was my calling and if it had not been for my stint in magazines, I would have never known it. You can't plan that; it just happens. People who tell you how they mapped out their five-year plan are full of it. You can't know. I'm sorry, you just can't. It's not a plan, it's a decision. Sometimes you make good ones and other times you don't. But the point is you're always the one choosing the direction.

I can appreciate how from the outside world, everything I was doing in PR seemed really superficial and silly. I recall how friends who didn't work in fashion used to say to me, "So, you get paid to play with bags and shoes all day?" Well, sort of. In PR, samples are your currency and I spent all day documenting, packing and shipping samples all over the world. The skills I now have as a cardboard-box assembler are really impressive; I'm equally talented with the duct tape dispenser; and as anyone in PR will tell you, it's likely that you will have a very unhealthy relationship with your messenger service, not to mention courier services of all kinds (WorldNet International is my fave). To get the job done, you need to do whatever it takes. And believe me, it takes a lot.

But it's also so much more than that. A lot of great skills come with learning the inner workings of an industry. It wasn't just that I played with bags and shoes; I was starting to learn how brands communicate a message through public relations, and more specifically through magazine editorial product placement. You can pay for advertising, but what we were doing was brand awareness the organic way.

When I started my career in PR at DKNY, the only people

we had to deal with were magazine editors and a few stylists. There was no online anything—no websites, no bloggers. (I know that seems like ancient history, but it really wasn't that long ago!) So you had to build your network in person or on the phone. *Gasp!* Likewise, editors had to discover trends independently; there were no sites posting "The Top 10 Trends from Fashion Week" in real time. Editors had to decipher the trends based on what they saw in person, without the added bonus of knowing what their competitors were covering. These days, if they really want to, they can just read up on what trends their competition is blogging or tweeting about.

There was also no practical way to track samples. Today we are spoiled thanks to companies like Fashion GPS, which offers a digital tool that can digitally track every move a sample makes, but back then, people used pencil and paper! (If you were really advanced, you might endeavor to keep tabs on your inventory via Excel.)

Even without proper systems though, we all seemed to make do, albeit inefficiently. For my job, it was really critical to know how a magazine worked—and in that area, I was covered. It was actually amazing how much I knew about PR just because I'd worked in editorial. **INSIDER TIP: Work at the opposite job to gain experience for the job you ultimately want.** It was the mirror-image perspective.

There really wasn't an accessories PR strategy to speak of when I arrived at DKNY. In fact, I don't think anyone there before me had actually focused on accessories exclusively. The great thing about that was that I was able to create my own way of doing things, and people welcomed it. In my mind, accessories were actually more important than people gave them credit for. I felt a real passion for accessories, something far beyond what I felt for clothing. Accessories were the solution to the ever-fickle fashion industry. Fashion trends move at the speed of light and though it's hard to rebuild an entire clothing wardrobe season to season, it's much easier to swap out a bag or shoe. I always say that I could wear the same little black dress every day as long as I could change my handbag and shoe options. Even more than the variety accessories provide, I felt the power (remember those Mary Janes that night in Bryant Park?) that a good handbag or shoe offered. Back then, there was no such thing as the "must-have" bag or the "it" shoe. But I felt it. I knew that accessories were the next big thing and that the accessories market would only get bigger.

So once again, I was faced with building a ladder where there wasn't one: I had to create a public relations strategy for DKNY accessories from scratch. I decided to base it on what I knew from the editorial side of the fashion business and then flip it backward. At a fashion magazine, I was on the "buy side." In public relations, I was on the "sell side." I had to promote accessories, but with what and how? So I asked myself what I found most useful on the magazine side.

My first order of business was to convince Amy that a visual lookbook of DKNY's accessories was a strategic way for us to secure greater press by making it easier for magazine editors to do their jobs. Previous to this idea, when editors came in to see the collections, they were meant to take their own pictures. But shouldn't we as PR people make it easy for them to reference specific items? So I took pictures of each accessory, had the film developed, and then laid out the photos on the color copier to print by theme (wedges versus heels, for example). For the cover, I color-copied an interesting print from a piece of clothing in the collection. My homemade lookbook wasn't super slick or even all that professional looking, but it was creative and it showed effort. No one had even asked me to make it; I just used common sense to identify a better way to do my job. If editors didn't know what accessories we had, how would they know what to call in for their shoots? This was one small example of taking matters into my own hands and creating a new way of doing something.

I made copies of my lookbook for every accessories editor at every magazine I thought should be featuring DKNY in its pages. I figured out the accessories editors' names by buying a slew of magazines and determining from their mastheads who covered the accessories market at each publication. Then I called each magazine to get that editor's direct contact information. I started a press list from scratch.

I built my accessories PR strategy from my gut. But without actual PR experience, how would I convince my boss that I knew what I was talking about? I have always believed that a good idea can come from anyone, at any level, but not everyone agrees. Some people focus on the person's title before the merit of her idea. That's a real shame.

So how do you present a new idea to your boss when you're the lowest man on the totem pole? And when? News flash: Your boss has the attention span of a fly. I have to admit, as an executive, I am guilty of this as well. I blame it on the fifty thousand things I have on my plate. But because of this, it's good to master the skill of boiling down what you have to say into succinct sound bites. If you only get your boss's attention for snippets of time, make a list throughout the day of questions you need answered—so that when you get your five minutes with the boss, you're as productive as possible. And before you start rattling off that list, always ask if it's a good time for him. That'll help your boss refocus, be in the moment, and in fact consider if he's got the patience to listen. But to be clear, if something is time sensitive do not wait until the end of the day to review it!

Take a Selfie: Are You Ready to Pitch Your Boss an Idea?

1. Did you do the research? I cannot overstress the importance of backup information. You can't just pitch an idea; you have to be able to explain the what, why and how of the idea.
2. Did you do competitive analysis? It's wise to show what your competitors are doing. That's a huge motivator. Make sure you include good stats to support your argument.
3. Are there à la carte options? People like choices, so present your boss with different scenarios. "If we do w, x will happen, but if we commit to y, I know we can get z." Oftentimes these different scenarios will have varied price tags associated with them too, so it's great to offer small, medium and large options. Presenting these differently priced scenarios also shows that you are fiscally sensitive and have put meaningful thought into your pitch.
4. Did you put it on paper? Presentation is everything. Put your pitch into a beautifully laid-out deck, complete with all your words and stats of wisdom. Even if you're rejected, your effort will speak volumes.

But how do you manage if your boss takes the idea you pitched and repurposes it as his own? I know it seems really unfair that someone who makes a lot more money than you do gets credit for your groundbreaking idea, right? But just like life, business isn't fair, so when that moment comes and you watch your boss present your idea in a group meeting, you have to suck it up. But don't fret! What usually happens after that moment of stolen glory is that people have questions—and that's where only you can jump in. Your turn to shine will come naturally. And when it comes time to execute the idea, of course you'll be the one taking the lead and bringing in different people to make that idea a reality. Having the patience to wait for that moment is key, because the last thing you want to do is interrupt your boss having a false "proud" moment.

Here's another idea: When you have a thought you want to share with your boss, email him about it. You've now created a paper trail that proves the idea originally came from you. (If it makes sense to cc people on the initial email, you can do that, but think twice—sometimes your boss may not appreciate it.) Save your correspondence in a folder entitled "Year-End Review." This is simply a way to protect yourself when it comes time to discuss your accomplishments from the past year. It's easy to forget everything you've come up with, so keeping a working file will save you at year-end. You'll be amazed at how much you've done!

Sometimes life is just like *Groundhog Day*. Different company, same problem. At DKNY, I was faced with a vast sea of shoe boxes that functioned as a closet, but with no organizational rhyme or reason. I couldn't see which shoe was inside each box, and it was impossible to do my job efficiently if I didn't know what accessories I had to lend at any given moment.

I decided that a visual inventory was the most sensible solution. So I shot a Polaroid of each pair and then pasted the Polaroid on the outside of each shoe box. There were a ton of samples per style, so I created a coding system that would detail what was in each box in the simplest fashion. I documented style name, color, material and size on each photo. But then came inventory. How would I know what was physically in the closet and what was out at a fashion shoot? I decided that the answer was double Polaroids, one on each end of each shoe box. One Polaroid would say "IN" and the other would say "OUT." This way, when an editor came into the closet to pull samples, I would remove the actual shoes, but leave the shoe box as a placeholder in the closet, turning it around with the "OUT" Polaroid showing. Once the shoes were returned to their box, I'd turn the box back around to the "IN" side. It was elementary, but it worked. It made me more efficient so that I could lend more samples for more shoots.

I was so excited by my little homemade processes, but honestly that's to be expected of me. Generally, I'm someone who gets excited when my closet is in perfect color order. But the thing was, I was excited beyond the organization. I was excited about what I was doing. I operated as if I had a little baby start-up with a product that was so genius, magazine editors had to shoot it. I had filled another void that would now allow me to do my job to the best of my ability.

MUST DO: IDENTIFY VOIDS IN YOUR BUSINESS

1. Think aerial view: It's often easy for us all to get stuck in the minutiae that we are tasked to do all day long. But every once in a while you need to take a giant leap into the air and look down upon what it is you're doing. You need a different perspective.

2. Examine the process: On any project, some of the things you do may be totally unnecessary. Cut the fat so you can refocus yourself on what is needed and allocate time for things you couldn't focus on before.

3. Gently rock the boat: I hate when people say, "Well, that's how we've always done it." Umm, who cares? Just because something has always been done one way doesn't mean it can't be done ten times better another way. **INSIDER TIP: Don't be afraid to question the status quo.**

4. Be a friendly neighbor! It's important to make friends with your peers at other companies. Obviously, you're not going to sit there and trade company secrets, but you can pick each other's brains on the innocuous stuff and probably learn something.

After tackling the lookbook and inventory situations, it was time for me to relook at how we stocked the magazines' fashion closets. An accessories editor could choose styles she wanted to order and keep exclusively in the magazine's fashion closet the entire season. When I was at *Atelier Magazine*, we had a huge DKNY shoe wardrobe. I'm sure the DKNY PR coordinator at the time thought that was a splendid strategy. *I mean, why not?* It certainly seemed like it made the editor's job easier. But for me, having been in that magazine's fashion closet, I knew better. Editors like fresh ideas, and those shoes began to feel and look like furniture after a while. They just sat there on the shelves waiting for the moment when they would be chosen, but the reality was they would never be chosen because they were the shoes that collected dust on the shelves month after month. The minute I got to DKNY, I decided that I would forever abolish the "shoe wardrobe" and make those editors start valuing the product that they had always taken for granted.

The first way to create demand is to make something scarce. I stripped every magazine of their precious shoe wardrobe and, as if on cue, they began to squawk and fret as to how they would go on without it. Since I was previously one of them, I knew their tricks and I wasn't about to fall for them. Sorry, people, you'll have to request my shoes just like you do Chanel's. There's a new sheriff in town.

Being the master of your own fiefdom is an exhilarating proposition. I loved public relations and I found it instantly gratifying. Nothing made me happier than hearing from an editor that a DKNY product had been shot. I wanted the collection to be everywhere; one editorial credit a month in each magazine wasn't enough for me. I lent samples for magazine shoots like crazy, but I was also relentless in keeping tabs on their whereabouts and their status. Was the bag shot? Can I get the bag back ASAP? I never let a sample lie idle. A sample that's just lying around is much more vulnerable to the infamous five-finger discount. I was averaging sixty accessories and shoe editorials a month, sometimes a lot more. I was so super-competitive with myself that I constantly tried to outdo my previous month's editorial credit tally. As time passed, I was able to get even more involved in the business side too, sharing editors' reactions with our sales team and trying to affect what styles actually ended up being produced and sold. I succeeded in proving to the company that accessories were the next big thing.

To get those editorial credits though, I had to pitch the product a lot, and pitching involved a ton of cold-calling. Every time I would call an editor and say, "Hi, this is Aliza from DKNY," I couldn't help but flash back to my days at *DC Moment* where I did that for hours every day and hated it. But in PR, I was on the sell side yet again, and just like at *DC Moment*, it was my job to make the first move. The difference though, is that this time I was able to build relationships and leverage them to secure press.

Knowing how to pitch is a requirement in PR, but to be honest, knowing how to pitch can prove important in any business. Whatever your job is, if you are trying to sell or promote something, it is an added bonus if you know how to create a promotion strategy. Preparing a pitch makes you consider what your "press hook" is: Why would the media or anyone receiving the pitch care about what you're saying? You have to be able to identify the selling points of an idea or a product in order to make other people take notice of it.

For example, I have a friend who works for a new health drink company. I hadn't heard of the brand, so I asked her if her company does any PR to generate brand awareness. She told me that since they were so new and small, they didn't have the budget to hire anyone. I couldn't help but put on my "PR hat" and started asking her questions about the product: Why was it special? What health benefits did it have? Did any other drink already do what this drink was claiming to? As she answered my questions, the "press hook" became clear to both of us. She immediately knew what would help her sell this drink and if she needed to pitch a journalist on the product, she knew what information she should highlight.

Take a Selfie: Do You Know How to Write a Pitch?

1. Do you know whom you're pitching? Journalists will tell you that what kills them the most is when they're pitched ideas that have nothing to do with a) the area they cover or b) the style of the publication or website they write for. You have to do the homework first and understand whose attention you are trying to get.

2. Did you identify your best PR angle? Are there multiple angles that can be pitched to different types of media?

3. Did you write a subject? I know that sounds silly, but a subject line is not only important to get a person's attention, it's essential later on for search functionality. Always make it easy for someone to find your email in the treacherous sea that is his inbox.

4. Is your subject any good? Adding an element of intrigue always helps, as does relating the headline to the reader. Words like "you" and "your" go a long way. **INSIDER TIP: Putting everything in the subject line gives the reader no reason to open your email.**

5. What email address is the pitch coming from? If you have a general email that gives off a spam

feeling, some might be less likely to open it. If your email has "asst" in its address, that might also be a deterrent.

6. Can you give an "exclusive" or an exclusive angle? People love the word "exclusive" because they love knowing that they're getting special content. Of course, if you use the word "exclusive," what you're giving/telling them better be.

7. Did you customize the content? You know those mass emails you always delete? Yeah, me too. People want to know that you really took the time to thoughtfully prepare a pitch. Don't kill it with those three evil little letters: "Fwd." Or worse, don't group email. The journalist doesn't need to know that you're pitching the same idea to a hundred other journalists.

8. How's your style? Sometimes it's not what you pitch; it's how you pitch. Humor and authenticity go a long way! If people feel like they are reading a mass pitch, they are going to delete it without giving it another thought. But always think about your audience and what is appropriate for whom you are speaking to.

9. Did you write a novella? Because if you did, no one is going to read it. Pitches need to be short and sweet. Ask yourself if you would want to read your pitch, because if you don't, no one will either. Remember that information is best digested in small, colorful bites. In fact, including pictures in your pitch helps a lot.

10. Did you follow through? It's not enough to have a good pitch; you need to be able to follow through

on what you promised in that pitch in a timely fashion.

11. Are you a stalker? Just because you pitch something does not mean the person has to respond or take action. Of course you should make one attempt (a few days later) to follow up and make sure your pitch was received, but if there's still radio silence after that, just let it be. Take no graciously and thank them for their consideration.

12. Were you gracious? Thank people who support you. It's not a given for them to do so.

The secret to pitching success is to have great relationships in place before you need them. As I built my career, I realized that the proof of a job done well was my true friendships with my editors. It's just like with your closest friends—you never have to say your name, because they know you and they know your voice. The warmth and trust that goes with that are the most essential ingredients in any successful working relationship. "Hi, it's me," is the ultimate sign of networking success. "Hi, it's Aliza," is the runner-up. This is the case in any industry. The friendlier you are with colleagues inside and outside the company, the more effective you will be at your job.

The reason relationships are essential to success is because sometimes it's going to be your job to promote an idea or a product that you know is really a hard sell. That's just the reality. So how do you do that? Well, you have to pull favors, and if you're not friends with the people who are ultimately in control of your success, then people are not going to go out of their way to help you.

Take a Selfie: Do You Build Successful Client Relationships?

A client is anyone you do business with. A client could be internal or external. Meaning, if it's your job to help your own sales team with x, y and z, then the sales team is your client. Client relationships are probably one of the most important things to foster and maintain.

Ask yourself these questions:

1. How easy are you to work with?
2. Are you accessible?
3. Are you reliable?
4. Are you credible?
5. Are you helpful?
6. Are you valuable to their business?
7. Are you indispensable?
8. Are you appreciative of their business? Do you show it?

If you needed three client references to vouch for you regarding the above points, would you have them? If the answer is yes, you know what you're doing! At the end of the day, business is about human nature more than it will ever be about business. **INSIDER TIP: People will go out of their way to do business with people they like.**

Shifting gears into public relations was the right move for me. I judged the position at DKNY on its future potential and where a career in PR could lead. It didn't matter that the salary was only slightly better than my salary at *Atelier* or that I was still doing many of the same tasks. I focused on the bigger picture of what new skills I could learn by being there.

Two years into my position at DKNY, I realized that I could be doing more. At the time, the Donna Karan New York PR person was handling both clothing and accessories. But since I was the one speaking to accessories editors all day, I knew that if I was able to also oversee Donna Karan New York accessories, in addition to DKNY, I could maximize their press potential. So I pitched the idea of creating the company's first-ever accessories PR department, where I would oversee both brands. The company was supportive. Thinking beyond the scope of my original job resulted in the actual expansion of my responsibilities. **INSIDER TIP: Showing your boss that you can build a ladder where there isn't one shows your potential.**

With my new role, I was able to be even more strategic. Owning the whole accessories market allowed me to really think about which magazines should be pitched Donna Karan New York versus which magazines were better suited to DKNY. But some magazines were important for both brands, and that meant my job was to convince those editors that they needed to give my brands double the real estate in the magazine. In those scenarios I needed to leverage my relationships.

In any industry, how you are perceived weighs heavily on your ability to succeed. If clients don't like to work with you, you're not going to get that promotion! Your reputation always precedes you, but the company you work for also contributes to that reputation. The companies listed on your resumé are like badges. People judge you not only for your skills, but also where you have worked.

A person's name can become synonymous with his

company. I call this "Last Name Syndrome." I'm sure we all know people who wield power by tossing around their company's high-profile name like a weapon. But if you rely too heavily on the influence of your company to bolster your position, it can also be a trap. You have to consider what your name will mean on its own when you leave that high-profile company.

When I moved over to PR and landed firmly on the sell side of fashion again, I swore to myself that I would never be a victim of Last Name Syndrome. After all, your name is to your job like platforms are to high heels. Sure, you can get around without them—but boy, will it hurt.

CHAPTER TEN

Text-Message Speak and Other Ways to Ruin Your Chances

OK, UNTIL NOW, I'VE BEEN YOUR SUPPORTIVE CAREER FAIRY WITH A PINCH OF SASS, BUT NOW IT'S TIME FOR ME TO VENT A LITTLE. RECENTLY I'VE SEEN OR heard several stories that scare the crap out of me. Ones that make me concerned that some people might not be properly prepared for the professional world. If you know these examples would *never* be you, go ahead and have a good chuckle while reading them. But if they might be you, I hope this will steer you clear of trouble in the future. If this feels like a mini–slap on the wrist, I'm sorry, I'm not sorry. But I can recommend a good moisturizer from Bergdorfs that can soothe the pain.

The good news is that we are lucky! Having access to so many people at our fingertips, thanks to the Internet, is a luxury beyond compare. When I was starting out in my career, I had the Yellow Pages. The Yellow Pages was my go-to, GIANT, multi-thousand-page directory (think diction-ary) full of businesses' phone numbers and addresses. Not only was it a monstrosity to comb through, the paper quality itself was horrendous—almost see-through thin. The odds of ripping a page as you were searching were high. The odds of not being able to find what you were looking for were even higher. So when I think about all the access we have now, from LinkedIn to Google and everything in between, I'm confident there is no excuse not to network.

As someone who is very engaged in social media, I love talking to all different types of people; especially those who are trying to break into the business and need advice. I am not saying that I'm the be-all and end-all, but I am one of a small population who is willing to give career advice to complete strangers for no benefit of my own. So it absolutely floors me how some people have literally slammed that door to opportunity shut. When people reach out to me via Twitter and ask if they could ask a few questions or maybe get some career advice, I always say yes. I give them my email or even sometimes my phone number. And guess what? Sometimes they don't use it. I don't understand it. How does someone just ignore an opportunity?! Just as bad are those who don't act in a timely fashion. You must cherish the fact that you have been given a chance and respect it.

You have to recognize opportunity when it knocks on your door, even when the opportunity is something as small as the invitation to email someone. Don't blow off chances to make a connection with someone who already has the job you want. And even if you're not entirely sure exactly what you want, you asked for a chance and someone is handing it to you and you're spitting on it? Don't do that!

But almost as bad as not seizing an opportunity is

completely blowing it by corresponding in text-message speak with someone you are trying to make a NEW professional connection with. One day someone I don't know on Twitter reached out for some career advice, so I gave him my email address. This is the email I got:

```
Hey, can u talk?
```

Really? Are we buddies? What he should have written is:

```
Dear Aliza,
    Thank you for agreeing to speak with me.
I would love to set up a time to talk that
is convenient for you.
```

Writing in text-message speak is a great way to show your lack of professionalism. I don't care if you spend all day in social media, you can't bring abbreviated words, slang and casualness into a truly professional setting when you are speaking to someone more senior than you are. To clarify, I'm not talking about when you are emailing your peers at work. If you want to end every line with LOL, LMAO or IRL, I'm cool. But that is not OK when you are speaking to an executive, pitching business or trying to network with someone whom you don't know personally. Being too casual with people like that can come off as completely disrespectful. This is especially true if you are dealing with people in other countries where the culture is different and they expect more formal communication. You get one chance, people. I'll go even further: You get one email subject line to even get that person to read what you wrote.

MUST DO: PROPER EMAIL ETIQUETTE

1. Think about your audience and the seniority of that person. Communicate accordingly. No one ever got into trouble for being too professional!

2. Never include a long list of employers or companies on a group email, even on bcc. It takes one person on that group to ruin it by not realizing that he's been bcc'd when he replies to ALL by accident. But besides that, if you want anyone to pay attention to what you are saying, you need to address each person individually and personally. That is, unless your email subject is GOSSIP, because everyone and their mother will open that one. *By the way, I've actually done that as a ploy to get colleagues to read emails. It works, but then when you don't have any gossip it sort of goes south. LOL.*

3. Proofread! Spell-check! Use full sentences and proper grammar with people you need to be impressing.

4. Correspond in a timely fashion. If you send an email to a potential employer or really any important email, don't go off for five days and desert your inbox. You need to be manning all your communication stations. People lose their appetite really quickly when they sense you're not on it. People who neglect their inbox for even a day need not apply for anything.

5. Don't stalk. But do follow up if you have not heard back.

6. Don't fill in the "to" section of the email until you're sure the content is perfect. Otherwise you might hit send by accident on a half-written or poorly constructed email.

7. Double-check that the person you are emailing is the right person. We all know so many people by the same first name, and it's too easy to send the email to the wrong John.

8. Keep it brief. People have limited attention spans. Couple that with how busy people are and it's a recipe for not wanting to read your email at all.

Here's another example: A guy recently asked me if he could include me in his fashion paper for school and I immediately said, "Sure, email me here." You can imagine my shock when I received this email message from him:

```
From: John Doe
To: Aliza Licht
Subject: Articles

Basically, with the article I'm going to ask
you a few questions. If you have pictures you
like to share that be great.
```

Even though this person didn't use text-message speak (good for him), this email is half-baked and unprofessionally written.

Here's how I would have revised his email:

```
From: John Doe
To: Aliza Licht
Subject: Interview request for student
fashion paper

Dear Ms. Licht,
   Thank you so much for agreeing to speak
to me. I am a [freshman/sophomore/etc.] at
[name of college] and I am writing an article
for my school paper, entitled X. My major
```

is communications and I would be honored to include you as a featured person. The process is simple, all you would need to do is answer the below questions:

    1.

    2.

    3.

    4.

    5.

Also, if you have a photograph of yourself that I can include, or any images that complement your answers, I would be happy to accept them. Please let me know if you have any questions. My deadline for responses is November 12.

Sincerely,

StudentX

Now, it's certainly worth noting that in the right situations, casual correspondence can actually help you make connections and influence outcomes. People enjoy friendly, entertaining banter especially when their inbox is filled with a slew of boring emails. But, and this is a big BUT, you just have to remember whom you're talking to, and it never hurts to draft something and then show a coworker or a friend first before sending. Ask yourself things like, "Is this too casual or comfortable?" or "Am I too junior to be speaking this way?" Think before you hit that send button.

So if you write professionally, you're out of the woods, right? Not so fast. Professionalism applies to lots of other situations, not just emails and cover letters. There are other technology pitfalls waiting in the wings. Here's an example:

Nick came in to interview for a junior position with Anna

at CompanyX. He was dressed very well. His look was clean-cut and classic. If you'd asked Anna, she would have said that he looked more like he was interviewing to work at a law firm than as an assistant in fashion. But OK, she'll bite.

During the interview, he spoke clearly and intelligently. His answers were on point and in general Anna thought he was great. They spent a while going through the position, and all in all she was convinced Nick was the hire for her. She walked Nick out of the office and toward the door, promising to be in touch with her decision in a few days. But in truth, she had already made up her mind to hire him.

When Anna got back to her desk, she decided to check Nick's social media profiles. After all, a resumé never tells the full story. She decided to look him up on Facebook first. The pictures she found upon searching his profile were shocking.

Anna wondered, how is it that in this day and age, people don't realize that your social media presence is Exhibit B, right after your resumé? Back in the day, your personal life would never come into play in a hiring decision, but those days are long over. **INSIDER TIP: The lines have blurred between what is personal versus professional.** If you want to post questionable pictures on your social profiles, then you better make sure your accounts are private.

After browsing Nick's social media pics, Anna's question became: "Can I hire a guy like this?" You may be thinking, how dare she judge his personal life! You might be angry reading this and you may be panic-stricken thinking about what you have online right this second that your boss may be seeing. Good. You should be. And if you have a job, if you list where you work on your social profiles, then what you post may be perceived as representative of the brand.

So was Anna going to hire Nick? Did she really want him representing her company? She decided the answer was no, but she thought it was only fair to check his references, since he'd interviewed so well. For starters, he had name-dropped several very senior people during their conversation. Easy check there, so she called them up and inquired about their friend Nick, whom they supposedly loved. Funny thing, not one of them knew who Nick was. One of his alleged references even decided to call his past employer to refresh her memory about their alleged work relationship. He had, after all, said that he had worked with her "directly" and "all the time." Well, lo and behold, it turned out that Nick didn't do anything of the sort. So now we also had a two-time liar. She decided that the evidence against Nick's stellar interview was too great to ignore.

There's a lot we can learn from Nick. This is just the way of the world now, so you have a choice: Either don't put questionable content out there socially, or make it private. Personally, I think the safest bet is not posting it. We've all seen way too many famous examples of celebrities thinking a text is private and then suddenly it's all over the Internet. **INSIDER TIP: If you put it out there, it can be used against you.** But the second issue with Nick is also very important: Don't lie about your experience or your contacts. It's just stupid and it's very easy to get caught.

OK, I feel a little bit better now that I've gotten that off my chest. I know that if you follow my lead, you will nail the interview process and get that dream job. But before you get really excited about your potential home run, there's another communications trap waiting for you when you get to the office.

George Bernard Shaw once said, "The single biggest problem in communication is the illusion that it has taken place." Isn't that the truth? But what Mr. Shaw forgot to mention is that sometimes communication happens, just using all the wrong words.

In an earlier chapter I wrote about the importance of knowing the players and understanding how to work with each personality type. But your boss is a different scenario altogether. No one ever teaches you how to speak to a boss. I, for one, had to figure it out on my own. But I've witnessed many people who have not received the memo. When I hear people use the wrong words or tone, it makes me cringe a little. OK, I lied; it makes me cringe a lot.

I'm a very direct person, and with that comes the risk that I'll say the wrong thing to the wrong person. I mean, it does happen from time to time. Hello, I'm only human. But over the years, as I have become a more seasoned publicist, I've realized that all messages—especially ones intended for superiors—necessitate strategy. There is more than one way to get your point across and some ways are just better than others. Here are some examples to demonstrate the two ways to communicate the same message; one, of course, is wrong.

Don't Say: "I'll get to that when I have time."
Do Say: "Can you show me what takes priority on my current to-do list?"

Don't Say: "That's not really in my job description."
INSIDER TIP: Your boss wants to know that you are passionate

about the success of the business, whether it's in your job description or not.

Do Say: "I've never done that before, but I am happy to."

Don't Say: "I'm so tired today." (Remember; filter what you say to your boss.)

Do Say: _____ (Nothing! Don't complain about being tired!)

Don't Say: "I'm really stressed out and I don't think I can handle this!" **INSIDER TIP: Always play it cool.** Talk to a friend or a trusted colleague, but do not share your stress with your boss. Your boss should always believe that you've got it all under control.

Do Say: "I have a lot of things I am working on right now, so can I finish those first before I take this on? Or would you like me to stop those projects and start on this?"

Don't Say: "That can't be done." Shooting down an idea before you really have had the chance to research it shows that you are both narrow-minded and lazy. There are very few things that are impossible. In fact, most things are possible. They might take extra effort and may require additional budget, but they can be done. In fact, I would say that most often when people say something can't be done, it's because they don't want to do it. Once you've exhausted all avenues, that is when you can safely declare an idea dead.

Do Say: "I will look into it to see what is possible."

Don't Say: "That's not my problem." Hello, if your boss is raising an issue to you, then she obviously wants it figured out. Bright side, she is giving you the opportunity to do extra credit. So rise to the occasion, lend a hand or a brain cell and get it solved.

Do Say: "Sure, I'm happy to take a stab at solving this."

Don't Say: "You never told me to do that."

Do Say: "I'm sorry, I wasn't aware that I had to do that." This way, you're not taking the blame for something that isn't your fault, but you have also managed to say the same thing without the evil word "YOU." **INSIDER TIP: Never point the finger back at your boss.**

Don't Say: "I left a message for him." No one checks voicemail as quickly or as often as they check email, so you can't equate leaving one voicemail hours earlier to really making an effort. If something is time sensitive don't leave a message. I would always go with emailing first and then following up with a call after if you don't hear back. But in general, waiting for someone to call you back is so ten years ago oh and P.S., it will NEVER happen. But just so you know, sending an email doesn't count for checking something off your to-do list either.

Do Say: "I've tried reaching him multiple ways and will be sure to follow up again shortly."

Don't Say: "I don't know." *I don't know* is basically throwing in the towel. You have to sound and be more proactive than that.

Do Say: "I will find out ASAP." Sure, that shows that you don't know the answer, but at least you're proactively going to do something about it.

Don't Say: "I deserve a raise" or even "I've been here two years and I think I deserve a raise." Time is meaningless. You need to show why you deserve a raise. No one likes an entitled person.

Do Say: "I would love the opportunity to walk you through my accomplishments this year. I think I have grown a lot in my position and I believe I am ready for more responsibility."

Don't Say: "I'm going on vacation on x date." Don't assume you get to choose the days off you want. You need to ask for permission first, and then book the time off.

Do Say: "Is it OK if I take the following days off? If so, I would like to book a vacation."

Don't Whine: There's a lot to complain about at work. Whether the coffee machine is constantly broken or your office cube is tiny, at the end of the day, bitching and moaning is not productive. Even though your boss doesn't own the joint and isn't personally responsible, he will be judging you based on how you act. Acting like you're too good for the office or deserve more can backfire. Your boss may take that complaining as a hint that you aren't happy and you want to leave. He might start mentally imagining life without you. Not a good scenario. Better to keep those kinds of comments to yourself.

Don't Be Socially Stupid: As a rule of thumb, and this bears repeating, check your company's social media policy before you post anything. But for certain, don't follow or friend your boss first (if at all). Always let her take the lead. It's awkward the other way around.

If you do follow each other online, keep in mind that there is a delicate line between boss/employee and boss/friend. So even though it's "out of the office" conversation, it's still important that you mind your words. Also remember that she might be watching what you say to other people and seeing the pictures that you post.

Don't Let Your Body Language Talk Too Much: There is no place for rolling eyes in business. Go back to the playground for that. In addition, whispering under your breath, sighing and chuckling are all rude and childish. Watch what your body does when your mind isn't thinking.

Don't Manage Your Peers: Sometimes your boss might ask you to do her dirty work. "Can you go tell EmployeeX that he needs to hand in that report?" That directive is fine and good if you are NOT the same level as EmployeeX, but if you are, you can't be giving EmployeeX orders unless you want to end up having him hate you.

Do Say: That you don't feel comfortable giving EmployeeX direction and you know that he would rather hear it from the boss. That also shows your boss that you understand the hierarchy and don't want to step on anyone's toes.

Do you see the differences in delivery? Just by changing the wording or tone you can severely avoid pitfalls with your boss. These are just some key examples, but if you can clearly see the difference in language, then you can apply the same principles to any other communication you have with your boss. These tips also apply to any executive in a company. You can't always just say what's really on your mind; you have to consider your audience. Oh and P.S., your audience generally doesn't want to hear it.

Can you tell that I'm really passionate about making sure no one makes these types of mistakes ever again? These examples upset me the most because they have nothing to do with talent or ability. They are penalties that you don't want to get in the middle of a potentially winning game; they're wasteful and unnecessary. Actions and words have consequences. Don't get taken out of the game before you've had a chance to play.

PART III

Rocking Social Media

CHAPTER ELEVEN

The Making of DKNY PR GIRL and Half a Million Followers

IT'S HARD TO REMEMBER MY LIFE BEFORE SOCIAL MEDIA, BUT LET'S GO BACK IN TIME, SHALL WE? IT WAS 2009 AND *GOSSIP GIRL* WAS IN ITS THIRD season. As a New Yorker, I couldn't resist taking in the over-the-top, scandalous lives of these rich, Upper East Side high schoolers and apparently I wasn't alone. In fact, I had to watch it live because I couldn't bear the thought of people talking about it the next day and spoiling it for me.

Gossip Girl herself was the anonymous narrator of the show, a character the audience knew by voice only. She spread her hearsay via text message to her many subscribers, which naturally included all the main characters on the show. She was always causing trouble and people feared being on her radar. The mystery of Gossip Girl's identity made for an intriguing, added layer to the show. Beyond this drama though, the fashion on the show, and specifically the styling, was amazing. I loved watching it for that reason, too—always looking to see what designer was being featured. *Gossip Girl*'s costumer, Eric Daman, worked with all the design houses directly. People cared what these characters wore and it was a great way for brands to generate meaningful press. (In fact, my admiration for Eric's eye eventually led to a collaboration—he designed a collection of hosiery for DKNY.)

One day at work we were in our usual PR/marketing meeting, when someone raised the topic of social media, specifically Twitter and Facebook. We were contemplating how and when we would embark on this next frontier of communication. It was definitely not my idea to talk about it; to be honest, I personally wasn't that into Facebook and I hadn't even heard of Twitter. But I'm always game for a new idea.

As we toyed with how we would manage social media, a colleague brought up the idea of "tonality," or how we would communicate on each platform. It was easy to decide that separate Facebook pages would convey the voices of the Donna Karan New York and DKNY brands respectively. But Twitter, as we understood it, was different. It lent itself more to real engagement and conversation, not just presentation. **INSIDER TIP: It's called social media for a reason. Engagement is everything.**

As I listened to everyone debating how to launch the brands on social media, I suddenly knew the answer: Public relations itself provided the perfect content to draw from. It was certainly a great vantage point into the world of the Donna Karan New York and DKNY brands. We worked with fashion editors, we produced runway shows and we dressed celebrities, among many other things—it would definitely be perceived as glamorous. I was sure people would enjoy being a fly on our wall. So I suggested PR as the filter through which we'd share our Twitter content—and the next logical question the group raised was, "But who would be the voice?" In that moment my mind immediately flashed to *Gossip Girl* and how her coy, mysterious persona was such a fantastic concept. I thought, *What if we took the idea of* Gossip Girl *and put a PR spin on it?* She could be a made-up character telling the brand story, and no one would have to know who she was. And I loved the idea of using the word "girl," because it was cooler than "woman." "Girl" is friendly and approachable. DKNY PR GIRL had a nice ring to it! **INSIDER TIP: Approachability leads to conversation.**

It was decided that I would be the only one to tweet because the content would be more controlled that way. Even though we were one of the first fashion brands in the social media space, with no examples to follow, we knew how important it was that the person managing the Twitter handle be responsible. Meaning, the last thing any of us wanted was an assistant taking the Twitter handle out on a Saturday night and going hog-wild on it. That happens; we've heard horror stories even of CEOs tweeting out the wrong things. Second, I was a PR executive and as such had a clear sense of what to say and what not to say. **INSIDER TIP: Filter what you say in social media. You never know whom you're going to offend.**

But besides all of the above, I had so much content to share. I mean, who didn't want to hear about how CelebX refused to sit next to CelebY at a fashion show because CelebY was a reality show star and CelebX was an acclaimed, real actress? *Duh, can't blame her.* Or perhaps our Twitter followers would be interested in CelebZ, who got a butt facial (yes, I said "butt facial") and had no shame stripping down in front of me to show me how it was done. Yeah, I'd say there was plenty to tell—all anonymously, of course. **INSIDER TIP: Anonymity can only go so far. Don't risk relationships for social media content.**

For the sake of brevity, the Twitter handle would simply be @dkny, not DKNY PR GIRL. We would use DKNY PR GIRL as the name on the handle instead. We purposely didn't make it @donnakaran, because we didn't want people to think that Donna Karan herself was tweeting (as brilliant as she would have been). That would be disingenuous, and we had an intuitive feeling that honesty and openness were the way to go in social media.

So who was this DKNY PR GIRL? Well, she was a completely made-up character. We came up with all of her likes, dislikes, hobbies, workout routines and places she frequents. She lived downtown in Tribeca and drank green tea just like Donna does. She was a yogi like Donna and liked cool indie bands. She was definitely not the Upper East Sider that Gossip Girl was, but that didn't matter. She was our version of *Gossip Girl* and she was brand-perfect.

For her look, our designer took my picture off my Facebook page (without my knowledge) and surprised me with a very stylized version of myself. **INSIDER TIP: The profile picture and bio in social media are like your resumé. Don't leave them blank.** By the time he got done with her, she had legs for miles (ahem, nothing like my stumps) and a very willowy physique; basically, a typical fashion illustration. I took that sketch and uploaded it to the @dkny Twitter account we made, then came up with the following bio:

> I'm your well-placed fashion source bringing
> you behind-the-scenes scoop from inside
> Donna Karan New York & DKNY and my life as a
> PR girl living in NYC.

I was very conscious about adding that last part—"and my life as a PR girl living in NYC"—because I really wanted our followers to feel her whole life, not just what went on during her workday.

So now I was ready. Twitter handle, *check*. Name, *check*. Bio, *check*. Now what? Oh yeah, minor detail: I didn't know how to tweet. I didn't even really know what Twitter was for. Have you noticed how I always seem to find myself in situations where I have to teach myself what to do? So I did. I decided that the only real way to learn Twitter was to just be on Twitter. I learned to tweet by watching other people tweet. There were some basic rules I had to figure out, but essentially it was just learning to write in short sound bites. How hard could it be? **INSIDER TIP: Tweeting is trial and error. Pay close attention to your tweets that generate engagement, and lose the ones that don't.**

My first tweet as DKNY PR GIRL was on May 8, 2009: "Fashionistas welcome to your front row seat! DKNY PR GIRL is now officially on the scene..."

Not my best tweet ever, but the first of anything is rarely very impressive. It got easier as I went on. What was so shocking about tweeting was how people were just out there, ready to respond. It felt like some alternative secret universe. It became addictive very quickly. Honestly, I started to feel like Twitter was my husband. It was the last person I spoke to before I went to sleep and the first person I spoke to when I woke up.

I'll never forget how my real husband, David, would totally make fun of me when I first started tweeting. One day while I was checking my timeline he said jokingly (but with a bit of snark!), "Oh, are you talking to your fake friends again?"

"They're not fake," I retorted. "They're real and I know a lot about many of them." He couldn't understand the allure, why I was "wasting" my personal time tweeting with people he considered complete strangers. As much as I would try to make him understand, he couldn't. I really couldn't blame him either. Chatting with strangers all around the world was not typical, but I explained that it was my job...until I realized that, in fact, no one was telling me to tweet at night, after work, or on the weekends. I was the one who felt compelled to continue the conversation.

So I went in and out of Twitter seamlessly while doing my "real" job as senior vice president of global communications for the company. Twitter became integrated into my life and I loved it. I still do. There's a certain sense of community and belonging that happens on Twitter. I like the idea of connecting with people and sharing common interests, like watching *Scandal* together and live-tweeting our commentary. You start to feel like you're on one giant, virtual couch. It's like this secret world that people just don't understand unless they do it. It's hard to explain to "outsiders."

Since I'm also a very off-the-cuff person, it was important for me to express my thoughts in real time. I never drafted content in advance. I felt more comfortable posting on impulse. No content calendars, no schedule. Every tweet was and still is spontaneous. I was lucky that the powers that be trusted my judgment enough that I didn't have to get pre-approval for my tweets. Of course they read what I posted after the fact, but the freedom to post about whatever I was feeling at the moment made for a very natural and open conversation.

Since Twitter was relatively new (very few fashion brands were even on Twitter at that time) and I had no experience on the platform, I had no idea that people would reply so readily and so often. The amount of people replying to @dkny's tweets started increasing at a rapid rate. One week we were at 210 followers, the next 10,000. DKNY PR GIRL had created a totally new way for a brand to communicate and we didn't even know it. The Twitter handle following grew exponentially from there.

The more I tweeted, the more responses @dkny got. I tweeted a lot, sometimes as many as sixty times a day. It was super conversational and really, really fun. I loved the insta-conversation. It was global and 24/7. I tried different tweets to test engagement. Would a tweet about the event I was attending get more replies than a tweet about a pair of chic new shoes? As weeks passed, I realized that the more personal my tweets were, the more people would engage. A tweet like, "Devil French fries at lunch, I just can't say no & neither can EditorX" garnered more engagement from our Twitter followers than me tweeting about the newest handbag that was now in-store. I studied the pacing and the reactions and I tried to keep the conversation going throughout the day. But I never posted just to post. I had to feel it. **INSIDER TIP: Be careful not to tweet too much consecutively or you will annoy your followers.**

DKNY PR GIRL had become a friend to those who followed her because they loved the fly-on-the-wall view she gave them. It was juicy. It was very insidery and very engaging. It was also a whole other job that I did on top of my real job, but I loved every minute of it.

The truth is, the idea of a fashion brand having a social personality—besides that of the designer—never existed before, certainly not beyond a company website or a catalog. Social media changed that. The "community manager" was a role that was just starting to evolve. PR people were always behind the scenes, sure. But the role of PR people before social media was to put out company statements—to be, in fact, the gatekeeper of the statement. They were always the messengers; they certainly weren't the main attraction. And when reporters would call asking questions, you'd better be sure that a brand's response was carefully crafted. Off-the-cuff tweets were not part of the job description.

But all of that got thrown out the window with the idea that someone was posting socially all day to the public. Even for me, this wasn't an easy concept to understand. The first time someone took my tweet and used it as a real brand quote in an article was shocking to me. It was almost an aha moment, because I never considered a tweet to be an official company statement. But of course, it was.

I'll never forget in 2011 when a cobra escaped from the Bronx Zoo in New York City. Someone cleverly created a Twitter handle for the escaped cobra, aptly named @BronxZoosCobra. The cobra's tweets were hilarious, adding a series of extra s's onto every word she could. I'm pretty much ten years old at heart, and was instantly enamored with the idea of a tweeting cobra, so I jumped at the chance to tweet at her. I didn't think much about it until a major news source included DKNY PR GIRL's tweet in a story about the cobra's Twitter handle. *Oh wait, was that like a company statement? Speaking to a pretend cobra? Oopsy.* Anyway, you get the point. A tweet was all of a sudden not just a tweet, a tweet was an "on the record" comment, whether we wanted it to be or not. **INSIDER TIP: If you wouldn't feel comfortable running a full-page ad of your tweet in the *New York Times*, don't post it.**

So Twitter life went on, and I got deeper and deeper into social media. If I was going to a fashion event, tweeting was easy because DKNY PR GIRL would simply be there "covering" it just like a journalist would. If I was in the office, there was a ton to talk about, too. I could tweet about fashion show prep or CelebX who I was trying to dress. Anything that went on, even normal office activities, served as content. Such as:

> Just came back from a two-hour meeting to
> an email inbox of hell. Please say I'm not
> alone?

> Pizza lunch today. Because you know, it's
> Friday and I deserve it.

> 3 p.m. face-plant into keyboard. Coffee
> anyone?

People saw tweets like these and could instantly relate, because the fact is that when you write something that resonates with everyone, people are more likely to engage. **INSIDER TIP: Not every tweet has to include an image or a link, and the shorter a tweet is, the more engagement it gets.**

But come Saturday morning, when I was really in the supermarket with my kids, I didn't know what to say. Could DKNY PR GIRL also be in the supermarket? Would she talk about such a mundane activity, something that had nothing to do with fashion or her job? My gut told me no, so instead I would tweet something like:

> Just took the best hot yoga class. Now
> starving. #WorkoutProblems

Which was much better than:

> Cannot get over how long the line at Fairway
> supermarket is right now.

For the most part it wasn't hard for me to come up with things to say as DKNY PR GIRL, because in my mind, her world was very clear. The hard part was writing it so it felt authentic, which was difficult because I wasn't really doing hot yoga—oh, and P.S., I have never done hot yoga in my life. (Side note: Way to ruin a perfect blowout.) I naturally gravitate toward being authentic and this pretend play didn't feel right for me. I tried to reconcile it by reminding myself that of *course* I wouldn't feel totally comfortable, because it *wasn't* me.

The more I tweeted, the more difficult it became for me to play the role of DKNY PR GIRL. People would reply and ask questions, questions that would get me deeper and deeper into conversation. For example, if I tweeted, "Loving my fall stroll in SoHo #ILoveNY," someone might say, "What street are you on?" Not that I couldn't pretend to be on West Broadway, but it just felt so disingenuous. (Plus, OMG, what if that follower was *also* on West Broadway?) I started to feel really schizophrenic and it became completely uncomfortable.

The thing was, people didn't understand (or care) that DKNY PR GIRL was supposed to be a made-up character. And of course, why should they? After all, here was a live person tweeting back to them, answering their questions. On top of that, people weren't stupid; they knew it was just one person tweeting on behalf of @dkny all the time because they very quickly got to know my personality and voice. The grand strategy we had created for Twitter was not entirely working out as planned.

So I went back to my longtime boss, Patti, to discuss possibly altering it. She understood my predicament and how it was hard to manage my alter ego. We decided that I would just tweet my own life anonymously as DKNY PR GIRL. That way I wouldn't have to say I was doing something when I wasn't. I just wouldn't disclose my real identity or tweet about personal things like my hubby and the kids.

By 2011, the @dkny community had organically grown to almost 380,000 followers. Some of those close to me knew I was DKNY PR GIRL, but they all kept the secret safe. The trickiest part became going out to fashion events. By this time many brands had joined Twitter, so if people were at the same event and also on Twitter, they knew DKNY PR GIRL was somewhere in the room. To not blow my cover, I would have to tweet in the bathroom or under a table, try ing very hard to keep out of sight. I also had to make sure to never disclose what I was wearing for fear of being dis- covered. Think about the irony of that—here I was a fashion publicist trying NOT to show off my outfit!

Twitter became second nature but there were other plat- forms, like Tumblr, that brands were also jumping on. One day, a Twitter friend tweeted, "@dkny why don't you start a blog?"

I responded with something pithy like, "A blog?!! I have enough to do in my day job, let alone on Twitter!" But his tweet gained traction and suddenly people were cheering on the idea. It was daunting. A blog? I had a full-time job in PR and had taken on tweeting 24/7 on top of that. Even though Twitter was technically a side gig, it was also super time-consuming. I didn't know when I would find time to do a blog, but I was also intrigued by the idea of having more space to play in. The thought of writing long form was excit- ing. **INSIDER TIP: Before you start a blog, determine what your purpose and point of view will be and stick to that filter.**

So we made the decision to build dknyprgirl.com on Tum- blr with the tagline "When 140 Characters Aren't Enough."

When I met with the people at Tumblr and told them I wanted to write long form, they told me that people don't like long form on Tumblr, that what they want are beautiful images. While I of course planned on posting beautiful images, I definitely wanted to use the platform to write. So I ignored them. My posts ranged from the principles of public relations to hard-core fashion and quotes I loved. Really, anything I was in the mood to blog about. It was fun to write and then I would use Twitter to get the posts "out there." My strategy was to write on Tumblr and chat about it on Twitter. It worked. **INSIDER TIP: If you don't have another social platform to use to drive traffic to your blog, stick to the content that is known to work best within the blog's platform.**

As time passed, between Twitter and Tumblr, DKNY PR GIRL became a popular online personality. Like Gossip Girl, she was a constant social figure, always there with an insider tidbit or to live-tweet an awards show. She was everyone's girlfriend and people really felt like they knew her.

But as the following grew, clients and other people we worked with started to get very curious as to who the person behind DKNY PR GIRL was. Our sales team would be in market with a department store and in the middle of the appointment they would stop and say, "Who is DKNY PR GIRL?! You have to tell us!" Sales wouldn't dare say a word. In a world where nothing is kept secret, no one spilled—a pretty amazing feat, actually. For two years, it may have been one of the best-kept secrets in fashion. I loved being DKNY PR GIRL, even anonymously, but it was really hard not getting caught.

CHAPTER TWELVE

Revealing Fashion's Biggest Twitter Secret

ONE DAY I WAS SITTING IN THE OFFICE WHEN MY PHONE RANG. IT WAS AN EDITOR FROM *TEEN VOGUE* CALLING ME ABOUT THEIR UPCOMING FASHION University summit, where they invite students from around the world to listen to some of the fashion industry's most accomplished designers. They were doing a panel on social media and wanted DKNY PR GIRL to participate.

I went to talk to Patti about it and see what she thought. I told her that I really wanted to speak on the panel, but that I didn't know how I could. I had gotten many calls like *Teen Vogue*'s before, but none of those had really moved me to perhaps finally reveal myself. This one was different. Maybe it was because it involved students, as I have always been passionate about mentoring, or maybe it was because I was tired of having a secret identity. The answer was probably both.

We decided to sleep on it and she would discuss it with the powers that be.

That same week, a producer pitched us the idea of doing a web series about Fashion Week. With the advent of digital everything, brands were, and still are, constantly searching for new content. So we did some brainstorming and thought that a look into the behind-the-scenes of Fashion Week was our most compelling story to tell. People who followed @dkny on Twitter knew what went into Fashion Week from a PR perspective, but to watch it actually happen on camera would potentially be an interesting experience.

We were producing three shows for that particular New York Fashion Week: a DKNY men's show, a DKNY women's show and a Donna Karan New York women's show—all while being followed around by cameras. It's one thing to be an actress, where your entire job is acting the part. It's totally another to have a real job to do while cameras hover over you, documenting your every move.

I'll never forget doing the Donna Karan New York show seating on camera. When you need to add a guest's name/affiliation label to the seating board, it usually means you need to move several more guests to make room for it (since each company sits as a team). Sometimes you start moving several labels and completely forget what you were trying to do, so you have to backtrack in order to undo the damage. So you can imagine how insane it was when we were making complicated moves involving multiple labels, and a producer would say, "That was great, guys, but can you do it again?" Are you kidding me? No, I can't do it again, I could barely do it the first time! We had hard work to do and quite honestly the cameras made it that much harder.

We shot all day for four days, and even though at times it proved really tiring and frustrating, there were tons of celebrities in attendance and great moments to cover. We were sure we would get plenty of amazing content to cut into the twenty three-to-four-minute webisodes.

A few days after the shows were over, I received the first webisode from the producer. It was the "show seating" segment cut into a three-minute portion. I couldn't wait to watch it. As I started to watch the clip, my excitement turned to boredom. It was painful to watch. Like growing-out-a-bad-haircut slow. I couldn't believe it. Here I was thinking how dynamic we all seemed while shooting and yet it fell completely flat. I didn't want to watch one webisode, let alone twenty. **INSIDER TIP: When it comes to online content, if you don't want to watch it, no one else will either.**

I ran into Patti's office to show her the footage and to see if she felt the same way. We passed it around to a couple of people on the team and everyone agreed it didn't have enough energy. We suspected that none of the other cuts would either, and it would cost a lot of money to try to see if they did. We decided it wasn't worth it. But now the question was, how to make lemonade out of lemons? The production had cost a pretty penny and it seemed really wasteful to just throw all the footage out.

As we were brainstorming on how we could salvage the video project, *Teen Vogue* called again to inquire if DKNY PR GIRL was willing to speak at the conference. Was I really going to go onstage and reveal myself as the person behind the Twitter handle? After two years of anonymity that seemed really anticlimactic.

But then it came to us! We could use some of the best footage to create a single, elevated trailer—or sizzle reel, as they are sometimes called. Then, we could use the short video to make the DKNY PR GIRL announcement in advance of the *Teen Vogue* conference. Kill two birds with one stone!

I called the producer to tell her about the new direction we wanted to take and that we had to move quickly to edit the footage into a fast-paced reel before the *Teen Vogue* event that Sunday. The producer said she'd have the final footage ready by Friday morning, which meant I would be able to get it cleared internally Friday afternoon and then launch it Saturday morning.

But these are not the kinds of things that pop into your inbox perfectly edited. In fact, there was a lot of work to do. For starters, it needed a narrative, so I went into the studio to do voiceovers and narrate the whole piece. Then I sat next to the editor to point out every edit we wanted. It can be really hard to articulate why something doesn't feel quite right, or why they can't cut from one point in the film to another because that's not how it would happen in real life. So I had to make sure my directions were clear.

By Friday afternoon the piece was as perfect as it would get given what we had to work with. I planned to upload the video to DKNY's YouTube page. Unfortunately, the person who normally handled that was out of town. But not to fear! He left me with explicit visual instructions to do the upload myself. *Perfect.*

When I woke up Saturday morning, I was super nervous and excited. I carefully laid out the instructions and proceeded to download the file. But wait, there were four files. HD this and HD that, all named differently. I didn't know which one was the final edit. I called the producer in a panic and she identified the correct one. But not so fast: When I went to watch the "correct" one, I saw mistakes in it that I knew for certain I'd already asked to be fixed. I called her again. Now I was starting to panic. As it happened, I had plans with my family that day to check out a day camp that was out of the city, and we had to leave within two hours. Finally, I figured out which file was "the one" and proceeded to start the upload process. **INSIDER TIP: Always review the content one last time before you post to ensure you have the correct file.**

"Your file will be uploaded in 2.53, in 3.45, in 2.42 hours." It kept on changing. *WTF?!!! Two hours?* I called the producer yet again, not understanding why I couldn't get a straight upload time from the computer. She explained to me that because the file was high-definition it actually takes a really long time to upload. *Is she kidding?!!* I didn't have that time. I had my kids pulling on my leg to go so we wouldn't miss the camp appointment. I kept saying "five more minutes" to David, as if I were pressing snooze on the alarm clock.

"Your upload is complete" were the sweetest words I had ever read. Finally! I loaded everyone into the car. On the road, I took out my iPhone and logged into our YouTube page. "Plug-in missing" were the words on the screen. *Plug-in? What the hell does that mean?* More panic set in. With the help of an emergency call to a colleague, I realized that I had not chosen "mobile" in the settings page. *Ugh!*

I fixed the settings and finally saw the video image pop up in the designated window. The video was ready. Now I just had to tweet it out. But I was scared. I was scared of the followers' reactions, scared that they would be bummed that the mystery was solved. I was fearful that they wouldn't like that I wasn't twenty-five and single (the way my voice naturally came off) and instead married with two kids. I didn't want them to be disappointed.

When I finally built up the courage and hit send on that

tweet, we pulled into the camp and I lost all the reception on my phone!!!! I had just posted the most important tweet of my career and had gone radio silent.

I proceeded to go on a camp tour for the next three hours with absolutely no clue what was happening on @dkny's Twitter timeline. *Did people like the video? Were they surprised? Were they disappointed? Do they wish they never knew DKNY PR GIRL's real identity?* My mind was going a mile a minute. As we walked about the campus, I distantly heard comments made by the tour guide, like, "And here's the pool." I had to hold myself back from screaming, "We know it's a f**king pool! Now speed it up!!!" I needed to get out of there and get those reception bars going on my phone STAT.

Finally, the tour was over and everyone piled back into the car. "Drive!" I demanded to David. I had to know what was happening on my phone. As we started to head farther and farther away from camp, the reception on my phone started to come back on. It was time to see what I had done. Was it the biggest mistake of my career or not? As the tweets started to load I could feel my heart beating out of my chest.

Reading fast and furiously as I scrolled through the thousands of replies to @dkny, I slowly started to relax. The response was exciting. People were of course shocked, but not unhappy-shocked. They welcomed the real me with open arms. I was happily surprised, but then I realized that in a way they already knew me. Two years of intimate engagement meant that even though they hadn't known my name or my face, they knew my personality inside and out. They knew my thought process and sense of humor. The face and the name didn't really matter, because to them I was always real, I just didn't know it.

From a PR standpoint, news of the "real DKNY PR GIRL" generated global headlines. I guess I really hadn't realized how big the secret was. People couldn't believe the person who sounded like a junior publicist starting out in the big city was really Donna Karan's longtime senior vice president of global communications—that "PR GIRL" was really a PR executive.

Looking back, revealing myself as the real DKNY PR GIRL wasn't all that scary, because my life was hers and her life was mine. Yes, I had been scared that people wouldn't like the mystery surrounding the persona being solved for them. By not knowing who she really was, they could imagine her to be anyone they wanted, and by disclosing my real identity, I took away that option. People were also floored that I was married and a MOTHER. I get it. But to many, that was also a welcome surprise. People were happy to see some career/life balance.

Now that I was exposed, I had to come to terms with the fact that my real identity would be attached to whatever I posted. It was important for me to try to forget that, though; I didn't want to let that influence what I posted. But when my actual name would start showing up in tweets in addition to @dkny, I always stopped for a second to digest the fact that the @dkny followers knew who I was. Tweeting behind a sketch had admittedly afforded me a lot of room to play, because it wasn't my face out there. It was "hers." But disclosing my real identity solidified my pledge to the public that they would get nothing but the genuine article from me. After all, being "human" on Twitter was one of the reasons that the Twitter handle was so popular. **INSIDER TIP: Transparency and authenticity rule in social media. People not only expect it, they demand it.**

Since 2011, being out in the open as the person behind DKNY PR GIRL has been the most exciting experience of my career. It affords me the freedom and honor to represent Donna Karan International at conferences and share all the insights I have learned over the years by being active in social media. I feel very fortunate to have been given the opportunity to create this social identity on behalf of Donna Karan New York and DKNY, two brands that I love. But without the amazing executive support I was given, DKNY PR GIRL's success would have never been possible. It's the authenticity factor that made it gain the traction it did. @DKNY's Twitter community today is over half a million followers strong, built totally organically. But probably even more importantly, DKNY PR GIRL has paved the way for many other brands to be "human" in social media, a concept that used to be foreign. Social media was once a novelty and is now a cornerstone in every major brand's communications strategy. DKNY PR GIRL continues to give fans an insider view into the amazing worlds of Donna Karan New York and DKNY—and on a personal note, my friends on Twitter continue to inspire me every day.

CHAPTER THIRTEEN

Being Socially Savvy

REMEMBER WHEN YOU USED TO HAVE TO CALL SOME-
ONE ON THE PHONE TO SHARE YOUR EXCITEMENT
ABOUT AN OUTFIT YOU JUST BOUGHT? I THINK WE
can all thank social media for giving us an outlet to post our
outfit #selfies, random thoughts and beautifully prepared
meal shots. But most importantly, in the age of the overachiever, social media provides us with the ability to connect with people without ever leaving the couch or office.

Don't get me wrong, no matter how great I think social
media is, it will never replace that in-person coffee, or even
that phone conversation, but it has remarkable networking potential that should be celebrated. Is it for everyone,
though?

People have vastly different opinions about social media.
Some people are addicted, some don't understand it and
think it's a waste of time, while others think it is the answer
to every promotional problem.

Here's the thing: It's not going away. But more than that,
it has changed the way people, companies and the media
communicate forever.

Social media can play a major role in brand building and awareness—whether personally or professionally. You can't deny the power of a globally networked, "always on" strategy. People crave social connections and commit hours to their favorite platforms. So if you want to build your network and personal brand, how can you avoid social media?

I know a lot of high-profile people who resisted the wave when social media came onto the fashion scene in 2009. They were above it, they didn't think they needed it and they couldn't be bothered. Now they're wondering what they can do to jump-start their social profiles, because they have realized how important it is for their personal brands. Recently a friend came up with a brilliant idea for a book. He pitched it and the publisher loved it. But the first question they asked him was, "How are you going to help promote it?"

He answered with a bit of surprise and annoyance, "Me? Isn't that your job?" Yeah, not anymore.

Social media has helped catapult seemingly regular people into personal brands. Hello, you're reading the words of someone who is a product of social media. Whether people realize this or not, what you post speaks volumes about you. That's a good thing. It's something that you can strategically employ to build your own reputation. Your social presence should be a carefully curated version of yourself. In fact, when we post, we are actually choosing to tell our followers something about ourselves, even in the subtlest ways. But more than just position yourself, social media enables you to craft your image just like a seasoned stylist.

As you become a content creator, you begin to think in a different way. You begin to edit and boil your thoughts down to marketable sound bites. It makes you succinct and direct. It makes you very aware of how you feel and what you are thinking. Thoughts like "Do I like this?" or "Ooh, that's pretty!" become highly amplified in the minds of the socially savvy.

People in social media are constantly hyper-examining their surroundings. One might argue that we're so busy snapping photos and editing text that we don't actually experience anything, but I would beg to differ. Pre–social media, do you think I ever contemplated the color of leaves changing in the fall or a gorgeously prepared dish at a restaurant? The flicker of a candle or the way the clouds move across the blue sky? Yeah, no. Say what you want about social media, but it makes those of us who do it take in the world in a very highly sensitized way.

It also makes you very knowledgeable about what your audience wants to hear and what they don't. You begin to learn what they expect and how to meet those expectations.

I'm not going to lie; I am personally biased toward Twitter. It's not that I don't love blogging or posting fun pictures on Instagram, because I do. But what Twitter offers me in particular is the ability to engage with people around the world in real time. It's a community in the real sense of the word. It also keeps me in the know. I get all my news from Twitter faster than I could ever read something in print or even online on a news site. Experts have argued that content is lost on Twitter because the volume of tweets is enormous and the timeline moves so incredibly quickly. That's true, but the best content always finds its place and its voice among your most ardent fans. If you post and then engage in real time, Twitter is the most intimate, global communication experience a brand can foster.

Social media provides a playground for everyone to put

parts of themselves out there. "How are you?" is replaced by "I feel." Social media has taken the waiting time out of expression. You can make the first move, and that's empowering. I'm pretty sure the concept of keeping something on your chest is obsolete. Now you can simply choose what platform to vent on. But before you start, you need to know what you're dealing with. Just like anything else, you need to know the rules of the house before you just stomp on in with your muddy shoes on. Over the years, I've learned what it's like to be immersed in social media. But to be clear, not just here and there but all day, every day. Here's how to be a gracious guest in the world of social media. Remember, when you're at a party this big, you better bring your manners—your personal brand depends on it.

MUST DO: BE SOCIALLY SAVVY

1. Find the platform—and the number of platforms—that feel right for you. If you don't have the manpower to manage being everywhere, it's better to start small and strategic. No need to force it. You don't need to be everywhere and neither does your brand, personal or otherwise. Master one or two platforms first and grow from there. Plan your strategy based on the kind of content you have to work with. For example, if you're not really going to have strong visual assets, then you might want to consider skipping Instagram until you do.

2. If you don't have anything good to post, don't post at all. Everyone will tell you that consistency in social media is everything. "They" say to post regularly and have a schedule. I have never followed that rule; that's just not how I roll. I

don't draft posts and I don't keep a content calendar. Every-thing I post is because I thought of it that second. If I feel like tweeting with people fifty times a day, I will. But that said, the more you post quality content, the more engagement you will get. **INSIDER TIP: Posting and engaging with your followers regularly will grow your following. You have to start the conversation and follow the conversation. Out of sight, out of mind strongly applies here.**

If posting on the fly isn't going to be feasible for you though, then do put together a content calendar that allows you to be in control of your message. For example, let's say you know that on Wednesday nights you're available to engage. Then why not plan to post on Wednesday night so you can hang around for the feedback? I don't like the idea of posting something important and running. To me, that's like putting a cake in the oven and then leaving the house. You need to make sure it doesn't burn.

3. How do you know what to post where? Sometimes you have a gorgeous photo, and sometimes you have an image that's not necessarily beautiful but serves to support a thought you may have. While a great image will work well on any platform, a not-so-great image might be best suited to Twitter because Twitter represents fleeting moments. I always ask myself, "Do I want to see this image again?" If the answer is no, it's going only on Twitter. If the answer is yes, I'll go one of two ways, Tumblr or Instagram. How do you know which of those two platforms to go with? Easy. Will cropping the image into a square for Instagram cheat your image? If yes, then opt for Tumblr, where the image can be showcased in full format. Of course, you could also opt for both! Facebook is a place that I reserve for special milestone moments. I'm not a big sharer on that platform, but

that's just my personal preference. Bottom line, post where you feel most comfortable and happy. **INSIDER TIP: If posting on a platform starts feeling obligatory, you shouldn't be there.**

4. Listen before you speak. Growing up, we were told to think before we speak, but in social media, you need to listen (a.k.a. READ). It's really important to know what conversations people are having before you chime in. For example, you may see a post that's actually the third comment in a conversation thread. It's always good to view the conversation from the beginning to get a sense of what's being discussed and everyone's sentiment. What you don't want to do is jump in and show everyone that you misunderstood the conversation.

5. Scratch other people's backs. When you can't think of anything original to post, try helping others get their thoughts out there. Giving voice to other people's posts by sharing them is a gracious move and one that's always returned in spades. It's also a great way to build your follower base. I bet if you post a link to someone else's post and tag them, they'll retweet it. People love a good humblebrag.

6. Don't be a robot. In times of a national or world crisis, you need to be on top of your social media profile. A great example: On the night Osama bin Laden was killed (hello, biggest world news maybe ever) there were fashion magazines tweeting things like "The 10 Best Lip Glosses for Summer." You can't live under a rock like that. It's perfectly OK to schedule posts in advance if that's what works for you, but leaving your profile unattended can result in an embarrassing scenario for you or a brand. There's nothing worse than not knowing what has happened in the real world. Personally, I believe that scheduling posts is the antithesis of what

social media is for. I also loathe automatic direct messages (DMs). If I get a DM that says, "Thanks for following! You can also like me on Facebook!" I literally want to unfollow immediately.

7. Embrace yourself. Don't try to fake out your followers by pretending you're invited to a party when you're not or name-dropping someone you're not friends with. Don't post stuff that doesn't actually belong to you. Not cool. Do, however, embrace yourself. You have unique qualities to offer the world and you just need to figure out which ones you want to put out there. The truer you are to yourself, the happier you'll be anyway. If you love to cook, for example, share some fun tips that position you as an expert. If you're someone who loves staying home and watching movies, why not become your own movie critic and post reviews socially? There are a lot of ways to prove your worth, and providing some kind of service to your followers is always a great tactic. Authenticity rules.

8. Don't beg. Do you beg for friends in real life? I doubt it. So why would you beg for friends online. Posting "Follow me!" is probably the easiest way to alienate people. How you build a follower base is the result of three things: 1) putting out great content, 2) engaging with the people who speak to you and 3) proactively reaching out to others.

9. The easiest way to strike up a conversation online? Ask someone a smart question or compliment something he has recently accomplished. People can never pass up the chance to say, "Thanks!" because it actually gives them an opportunity to highlight their achievement without outright bragging.

10. Seek out your business. For my line of work, I'll often go into the search function on Twitter or another social media

platform and look for keywords that relate to the fashion industry. One day I checked for "shoes" and came across someone seeking a new pair of black shoes but who had no idea what to buy. I decided in that very moment to make her a Pinterest board filled with nine different styles of black DKNY shoes. Not only was she surprised and delighted that I took the time to do that just for her, she ended up buying two pairs. As an individual, your followers also want to gain something for following you. If you have great advice, or a good fashion eye in this case, why not recommend something? The more you speak about a subject intelligently, the more you can become an "expert" on that subject.

11. Keep the "social" in social media. Duh, there's a reason it's called social media, you know. I truly believe that the more friendly and open you are to the people speaking to you, the bigger your community will grow. If you take the snob approach and fail to engage people, trust me someone else will end up engaging them instead.

12. Play nicely in the sandbox. Brand-to-brand love, even with a competitor, shows that you're confident and comfortable in your own skin. Microsoft congratulated Sony on its PS4 launch, and Sony reciprocated the friendly banter with a similar sentiment as Xbox was set to launch the week after. What that did was make the public feel like the companies and the executives on each team were actually friends. It made both brands likeable. The same can go for industry colleagues. It's OK to show the world that you are not competing with one another. It just makes you look that much more powerful!

13. Content is king. People love using this phrase. What it really means is, the more ways you can come up with to enhance your brand—without outright selling anything—the better.

Except for on Super Bowl Sunday, people hate watching commercials, so you can't bombard them with ads or sponsored content on your timelines. **INSIDER TIP: Sprinkle the commercial in every once in a while but the rest of the time, tell a really good story.** What's the history behind something? How did your brand come to be? What's a crazy or funny tidbit you learned along the way? There are lots of ways you can go; think fly-on-the-wall, behind-the-scenes stuff. The point is, come up with interesting content that enhances but doesn't blatantly sell.

14. Inspire! People love to be inspired. That's why quotes, whether motivational or encouraging, go a long way in the social space. Quotes are pretty much a given to be retweeted, which will grow your audience exponentially. While there are tons of ways to find quotes all over the Internet, I think the best quotes are the ones that naturally come from you. Any piece of advice can be turned into a tweetable quote. For example, one morning I was getting dressed while my son was in the other room listening to the song "Life Is a Highway" as featured in the movie *Cars*. I instantly thought to myself, "Life isn't a highway, it's a runway." So I posted it as my own quote. People reacted to the tweet with comments like, "Yes!" or "Thanks for that, I'm going to clean out my closet now." The tweet motivated people to think about how they present themselves in a different way: Life is a grind, but that doesn't mean you need to show it.

15. Don't show up for every fight that you're invited to. People tend to get a little aggressive online. It might have something to do with the fact that nobody is face-to-face. And let's not forget about the Internet trolls, whose sole purpose is to create havoc and upset in order to elicit an emotional

response. You must use every ounce of strength in your body to ignore them. No one ever wins when they fight online. It just explodes. People chime in on both sides and things get really ugly. Don't go there. It's not worth it and you won't win. And on the flip side, don't start drama by tweeting something flammable, because it will catch fire and that fire won't be easy to put out. As for political, religious or racial issues, always tread carefully—or better yet, don't go there. These topics bring out a host of feelings and are a hotbed of tension. It's also wise to not post negatively about celebrities who have fanatical followings. Those fans mean business and they are relentless in their loyalty.

16. Enough about me, let's talk about me. I get it; we share a lot about ourselves. But you have to be careful about how much. Bragging is not a good quality, offline or on, and though it's normal to get excited about things, just remember that not everyone has the same luxuries and luck that you might. Be sensitive to that. Humility is always a more attractive quality.

17. Think like a PR person. There are many things—especially things in the workplace—that are completely proprietary. Those things are completely off-limits to post. I've said this now several times in this book: It's always best practice to familiarize yourself with your company's social media policy, as every company has a different approach to social media in the workplace. Can you tell I'm super serious about this? In general though, just like Vegas—what happens in the office should stay in the office, unless it's your job to share it.

18. The myth of the delete button. Yeah, this is a tough one. The delete button is technically there, but the truth is that in the amount of time it took you to delete a post, some evil person

out there is laughing over the screenshot they just took of it. Words live on forever. **INSIDER TIP: Pretend the delete button doesn't exist.**

19. If you build it, they will come. Imagine preparing a gorgeous dinner party, but only once the table was set and the meal ready to be served do you first start thinking about whom you should call to invite over and experience it. That would be silly! You have to do the inviting first, and then cook the meal. The same goes with social media. It's important to build a community before you need one. Establish your network well before you want them to experience whatever it is you want to put out there. It won't work the other way around.

20. Find your honorary PR people. Why not contact some of your socially savvy friends offline or privately and ask for their support as you build your network and get the word out? Nothing is better than third-party credibility, so help others help you share your news. Besides, the more varied the sources that a piece of news comes from, the more credible it is. Sometimes when someone asks me a question about a DKNY product, instead of answering it myself, I will throw it out to our Twitter followers to answer. Hearing from the public, especially since they don't actually work for the brand, is way more powerful than me saying I love this or that DKNY product (even though of course I do). On the personal side, if you're trying to drum up support for a new project, for example, the same advice applies. Offline requests for support can result in online promotion from your biggest supporters! People don't always need to know about the elves working in the toy shop, you know...

21. Curate your timeline. You need to watch the order in which you are posting. For example, retweeting five times in a row

might give off the idea that you don't post original content. I believe in an eclectic timeline. Start with posting original content, then respond back to some comments and finally share other people's content. You want to show that you are both speaking and watching the various conversations throughout the day. A good test is to check your timeline once in a while and see if you think it would look good to someone who doesn't know you. If you find that you are posting too frequently, why not just "favorite" or "like" a few posts instead? Too many consecutive posts feel like spam and will result in unfollows. For other more visual platforms, just make sure you're not overdoing the same type of post, unless of course that's your niche, then by all means . . .

I'll never forget Julia Roberts in the classic movie *Flatliners*, when Kiefer Sutherland said to her, "You lied to me," and she said, "I didn't lie to you, I just didn't tell you." He replied, "Withholding information is the same thing as lying!" I don't know why a line like that from a movie I saw when I was a teenager would stick with me, but something about it made me really think.

For two years as the anonymous DKNY PR GIRL, I let the world believe that I was this twentysomething single girl living in New York City. I didn't say that I was in my twenties and I didn't say that I was single—but I also didn't say that I wasn't. Was I being dishonest by not showing all my cards? Sometimes I felt like I was. But it wasn't appropriate to share more. The time wasn't right.

For those two years I felt very much like a secret agent. I was tweeting about dinners and parties that I was going to, then going over to Facebook and posting pictures from my children's first day of school or a family vacation. I actually loved the duality of having both, of not having to choose one or the other. **INSIDER TIP: If you manage multiple handles on the same platform, always pause and consider if you're posting the right content to the right handle before you do.** I guess I could have started an @AlizaLicht Twitter handle back then and used that for personal stuff, but I was so engrossed in being DKNY PR GIRL that I felt people would realize the voice was the same and my secret would be revealed.

But in 2011, when I revealed myself as DKNY PR GIRL, people became privy to my personal life, too. In the *New York Times* article titled "P.R. Girl Revealed as P.R. Executive," all my little secrets came tumbling out: the husband, the kids, where I was from, where I lived, the whole kit and caboodle. My life was now an open book. But it didn't make sense for me to talk about my family life on DKNY's Twitter, so I kept the two worlds separate.

Since I put so much of my personal life on the @dkny Twitter, I really had to find a different purpose for @AlizaLicht. @AlizaLicht had to be the other side of the coin. So when I finally started my @AlizaLicht Twitter handle in 2012, that was where, for the first time, I had a place to talk about my family life if I chose to. People knew me so well from @dkny, but they didn't know me as a mom or as the school Parent Association president. It was important for me to show people the other side. People who don't have families always wonder about how one strikes a balance and manages to fit it all in, and I thought by giving more of that part of my story, it would encourage people to take on more, in whatever areas they wanted to.

Friends and colleagues alike follow my personal accounts, and it gets harder to keep track of who may be watching and reading my posts. If I put something out there, anyone can see it. An editor I just pitched a story to can go read what my daughter said to me when we were rushing out the door that morning.

The fact is that when you have a social profile, your professional colleagues can read about your personal life. And guess what? They are judging it. I know people love to say, "Oh, but that's my personal page." Yeah, that doesn't matter anymore. Nothing is sacred unless you make it sacred. The bottom line is that social media has broken down the wall between what's professional and personal. So I am very calculated and very strategic about what I put out there. I may tweet off-the-cuff, but I always think before I speak. I don't know who might be following along.

I also can't just mouth off, no matter how much I would sometimes like to. That's a really strange feeling. But if you want to be successful, you can't just mouth off either. How you represent yourself matters. You can no longer hide behind the "oh but that's personal" excuse. **INSIDER TIP: If it's really personal, then don't put it out there.**

But there's another way to look at it. If the lines have blurred between where professional ends and personal begins, why not make the most of that? Everyone loves to be a fly on the wall and if you are a dynamic professional, it's actually interesting content to show some behind-the-scenes views of your personal life. Think about how much we love getting a tour of a celebrity's home on the E! channel. So why not purposefully offer people that backstage peek? The trick is to have it marry nicely to your professional side. For example, if you're a really buttoned-up professional, I don't want to see that you live in a mess of a home. That will make me think, "Wow, maybe she's not as together as she looks." **INSIDER TIP: Don't shatter your professional image by sharing the dirty little secrets of your personal life.**

What you want to share from your personal life is something that complements your professional image. Think of each piece of content that you share as a puzzle piece. Ultimately each puzzle piece needs to fit together to create the overall picture. That picture is you and your personal brand. Now you may be thinking, "I don't have a public image!" But you do. Anyone you interact with outside your home is consuming your public image. Whether you're a professional working in an office, a mom volunteering at school, or a student interning at a company, everything you do contributes to your public image. **INSIDER TIP: You are 100 percent being judged.** If you are trying to build your profile socially, you need to enhance it with things that continue the message in a cohesive way.

The Coveteur is a fashion website that gives people glimpses into the personal style worlds of many influential people. They have a genius strategy for doing so in a way that doesn't involve these massive double-page-spread photo shoots. What they cleverly do is shoot little, tiny vignettes of a space. So maybe it's a shoe sitting on top of a pile of books, or it's a lipstick sitting on a vanity table next to a gorgeous bouquet of flowers. It's rarely the whole room. It's a moment. They shoot many of these really tightly cropped and edited vignettes and create a collage of the person's life. It ends up painting a really pretty personal picture without showing it all. I love that strategy and I think it very much applies to what you can choose to show personally in social media. Little creative snippets. Not the whole deal.

Social media is a strategic weapon to help you build your brand—whether personally or professionally. It's the most effective way of networking and connecting with people around the world on a vast scale. The statistics on social media are staggering. I won't bore you with the details, but just know this: You can't have fun if you never go to the party.

CHAPTER FOURTEEN

Social Media Damage Control

AT A GREAT PARTY, SOMETHING ALWAYS BREAKS. LIFE ISN'T JUST ABOUT THE SUCCESS STORIES; IT HAS TO BE ABOUT THE FAILURES, TOO. PEOPLE DON'T LIKE TO see perfection all the time. They can't relate to that. They want human beings, and human beings mess up. I'm not suggesting you flaunt everything you've done wrong to the world, but every now and again throw out something that makes you human. You know, for good measure. **INSIDER TIP: Mix three cups of success with a pinch of failure.** Besides, if you're being open about a process, sometimes when you fail, you have no choice but to fail publicly. So how do you do that gracefully?

In the weeks leading up to every awards season, I always tweet about the ins and outs of celebrity dressing. The tweets are teasers referencing "CelebX" and "StylistX" so that people can understand the blood, sweat and tears that go into trying to get a celebrity to wear a gown on the red carpet. In fact, one of the main reasons I tweet about the process is because if by some chance we fail, nothing makes me crazier than people asking us on the Monday morning after an awards show, "Why didn't you guys dress anyone?" (As if we didn't try?!!) Don't they know how hard we worked to NOT dress someone? How many rounds of decisions and fittings we have to go through just to NOT dress that celeb? Of course they don't. Truth be told, I think if celebrity dressing wanted to be a competitive sport, I'm pretty sure that it has a shot at the Olympics. For the most part, we do very well on the red carpet, but sometimes things just go awry.

One year, though, I was very certain that we would succeed. We had a celebrity confirmed early to wear a custom Donna Karan New York gown. It was designed to measure for CelebX and she loved it. We were ecstatic! Getting a confirmation early takes so much pressure off and sure beats stalking E!'s red carpet coverage to see if someone decided last minute to wear a Donna Karan New York gown. Every time I think about "chance" in those scenarios, I think about how painful it is to have to depend on chance, but that's just the reality. Celebrities have soooo many choices of which gown to wear. In fact, no demonstration of excess ever struck me so poignantly as when earlier in that same awards season, CelebX tweeted a picture from her Golden Globes fitting; she had sixty gowns to choose from. I spied a Donna Karan New York gown in that photo—it was red and dead square in the middle of four racks of options—but becoming the "chosen one" that day proved to be an impossible feat.

But this time, I didn't have to think about all the other choices CelebX had. We were confirmed as THE one. *Phew.*

Our dress fittings with CelebX went well leading up to Oscar Sunday. I was also very close with CelebX's stylist, who I felt was always up front with me about when a dress was working and when it wasn't. I had kept @dkny's Twitter followers up to speed through the whole process, and they knew that we had confirmed CelebX to wear our gown. To be clear, when a stylist uses the word "confirmed," that's a big deal. In the world of celebrity dressing, "confirmed" carries a lot of weight, and people don't just throw that term around lightly. So I was beyond ecstatic and thankful, because P.S., she was our only chance at having someone on the red carpet that night.

At six p.m. that Sunday, I set up command central in my apartment as I always do before an awards show. I was so excited to see CelebX grace the carpet in Donna! My attire was my usual pull of comfy pajamas, just as my event "venue" is always my couch, and I'm always armed with frozen yogurt and two laptops, ready for battle. One laptop is for my media alert to the press, which includes the description of the gown and who we have dressed. The other is to host @dkny's "Twitter party" and monitor the social conversation.

I always draft the media alert early—as soon as I have confirmation on which celebrity is wearing what—but I never hit send too early. That can be a disastrous example of pulling the trigger too quickly and could result in excruciating embarrassment. Boasting that you're dressing CelebX and then seeing CelebX show up in another designer's gown is pretty much a fashion publicist's worst nightmare. As such, my finger always hovers over the send button while my eyes eagerly await that moment when I first spot CelebX on the red carpet during E!'s pre–awards show coverage.

As my finger hovered over the send button that year, my mind debated whether to press it or not. "She's confirmed," I reasoned to myself. "Just hit send!" But the other part of me was nervous. What if something had happened and CelebX had changed her mind?

E!'s red carpet was in full swing and I couldn't take my eyes off the TV or @dkny's Twitter feed. I hadn't breathed a word yet, on Twitter or anywhere, as to exactly which celebrity we were dressing, but I had insinuated that it was someone MAJOR. With my finger still above the send button, I quickly scanned the television for signs of CelebX. Suddenly I saw the top of her head among the sea of celebrities and publicists populating the carpet. As she came closer, I realized that she was not in the platinum sequins I had been counting on, but in another totally different gown. She was wearing another designer!! I couldn't believe my eyes. She was not in Donna Karan??!!! WHAT?!!! How could that be?! She was CONFIRMED. But there it was, clear as day on the red carpet. My worst fashion nightmare had come true.

I stared in complete shock and disbelief. I was destroyed. Not only had I mentally counted on her, but I had spent weeks hyping it to the public as well. I was embarrassed and so upset. Everyone who followed @dkny on Twitter was going to figure it out. They knew how CelebX's fittings had gone and they knew our gown had been among those in the running as CelebX made her final decision on whom to wear. They knew all this because I'd tweeted about it. And when CelebX's stylist had "confirmed" (I have to use quotes around that word now), I had tweeted that. We were a public failure. Now what?

As I sat there drowning in my misery, I watched countless tweets scroll past saying things like, "Hey @dkny who did you dress?" Since I was live-tweeting the show, it's not like I could go roll into a ball in the corner of my apartment and just disappear. I had to face the music and I knew I had to respond. Just as it always is, I knew honesty was the best policy.

I decided, what's the worst that could happen if I owned

up to the failure by tweeting a picture of the gown that *wasn't* worn to the Oscars, the dress that CelebX *almost* wore? So I did. In about two minutes, the photo of the gown that didn't make it to the Oscars racked up more than 2,200 views, with full-blown discussion about whether CelebX would have looked better if she had worn Donna Karan New York. My Twitter friends felt my pain and by being open about my failure, I had managed to create press and buzz about the brand by talking about something that didn't *actually* happen.

Sharing a failure publicly was an odd yet liberating feeling. What I realized from that experience was that failing doesn't always have to be negative. Sometimes you can turn failure into an opportunity to do something else.

But we all know that's not always the case. Remember that very famous phrase "all press is good press"? I am sure that if you ask any publicist today whether they still agree with that concept, they will tell you NO WAY. Crisis management in the age of social media is a nightmare. Let me tell you a cautionary tale.

Steve was a partner at a prestigious law firm and gave off an air of total professionalism. But in his personal life he let off steam via an anonymous Twitter account. There he could rant about politics, sports or really whatever was on his mind. Steve was very opinionated and sometimes his tweets would be heated and offensive, but his following was small and, after all, no one knew it was actually him, so there was no harm done. The anonymity gave him a license to say pretty much whatever was on his mind.

Until one day a particular tweet gained a lot of traction. His small following gave way to hundreds of retweets and the tweet took on a life if its own. But Steve wasn't worried, because no one could possibly know he was behind it. Steve gained hundreds of new followers, which made him realize that the more vocal and argumentative he was, the faster his following would grow. So he kept at it and, of course, it became addictive. Steve would weigh in on any news issue, giving his commentary like a seasoned, very argumentative news reporter. His Twitter handle became very, very popular. It was his little secret and it was fun!

But one afternoon, he got a surprising email from a colleague who asked, "Are you the person behind *that* Twitter account?" The question made Steve stop breathing for a moment. How on earth could anyone know? Steve started to panic. At this point his following had grown to thousands and he wasn't keen to give up his secret social profile. He decided to ignore the email and pretend he never got it.

Gossip began to ensue around the office kitchen, but no one said anything directly to Steve. But then something happened. Somehow unbeknownst to Steve, someone had tipped off a gossip site that Steve was the person behind the popular and controversial Twitter handle. He found out the old-fashioned way (*S), by reading about himself online. He could not believe that he had been caught. With the news out, social media timelines everywhere blew up and all eyes were on him.

Reporters were quick to troll through his timeline, screen-grabbing as many inflammatory tweets as they could. Steve promptly deleted the account (which by the way seems to be every person's poor solution to a social media crisis), but it was too late. The damage was done.

The power of social media, right? More like the frightening world of social media. Cue the theme to *Jaws*. When people refer to things going viral, this is exactly what they mean—and viral is not always a good thing. The law firm could not tolerate having a controversy around a senior partner and asked him to step down. A little secret Twitter account destroyed his career.

This story, as well as many other examples of social media crises you can look up, proves once more how what you do personally can affect your professional status. Steve did put out an apology statement but it was too little too late. The fact is that no social media profile is worth risking your status or profession, as tempting as it may be to post whatever is on your mind. But if you don't heed this warning, you better be ready to manage the aftermath.

Crisis management, especially in social media, is crucial. It's not enough to be savvy at posting content that generates high engagement. If you are not skilled and ready to execute a crisis-management strategy, your brand, whether personal or professional, can be destroyed in minutes by not being prepared.

MUST DO: SKILLFULLY MANAGE A SOCIAL MEDIA CRISIS

1. Craft a well-thought-out statement. Don't be hasty! Make sure you have ALL the facts. You should never, ever comment on something if you're not entirely sure what happened. While you wait to gather information, if your social media timeline is heating up, you could put out a statement like, "I am in the process of learning all the facts related to this incident and am doing everything I can to rectify this situation." Basically, craft a placeholder statement that shows people that you are listening.

2. Mind the clock. I don't know how this happened, but I guess because social media moves at the speed of light, people expect a statement or apology to be issued just as fast. Try to be as timely as possible.

3. Empathy, empathy, empathy! Be humble when drafting your apology. Just like everything else, the apology itself will be judged. Was it sincere? Was it defiant? Did you really take responsibility or did you shove the blame on someone else? There are a lot of things to consider and the most important of all is, will your apology be meaningful? Will they want to forgive you and move on?

4. Blame is lame. Seriously, I know it's tough to swallow many a pill, but sometimes you're just better off owning the mistake. If you simply say, "I'm sorry," there's very little to criticize. But if you say, "I'm sorry but x, y and z happened and I had no choice but to a, b, c, blah, blah, blah," it's all NOISE. All anyone will see in that apology is that you're only sorry you got caught. That is not what you want.

5. Get your apology out strategically. Most crises are discovered in social media first. So when you post your apology, post it first on the platform where you discovered the situation. What you don't want to do is put it across all your social platforms and cause people to learn about a mistake they didn't even know about. Of course, if what has happened has been covered in the news media on all levels, then by all means blanket your apology everywhere.

6. Babysit your crisis. You need to be monitoring the press and all your social platforms 24/7 during a crisis. Read the posts and comments on all your platforms. You need to be aware of not just what people are saying TO you, but also ABOUT you.

7. Understand whom to answer. I find the people who attack most on Twitter and post the nastiest comments on Facebook and Instagram are generally people with small followings. As I have mentioned before, there are also the trolls who live to cause a stir. Be careful whom you respond to in a sticky situation. You will never win with some people, and you can generally know who those people are just by taking a minute to read through their personal posts. One of my most favorite things to watch during a controversy is the infighting between fans on a timeline. There will always be one or two super-vocal fans who do the fighting for you; let them.

8. Let the apology sink in. I always feel it's important to let an apology settle for a bit before you go on talking about other things. So wait a few hours before starting to post on different topics. As you resume regular posting, your apology will inevitably be pushed down your timeline. That's OK. Just don't ever delete it! The social community has a thing about deleting things that make people feel uncomfortable.

All of the above tips apply to company brand managers too, with the additional points:

9. If you have a Facebook "fan" page for your personal or professional brand, it's important that you can control the message without taking away the voice of your community. Deleting comments in social media is a big no-no. In order to get around that, you need to establish community guidelines. Community guidelines outline what language you will not tolerate so that when people don't follow your house rules, you maintain the right to take down their comments.

10. Assemble a crisis team—and a crisis to-do checklist—before you need them. It's imperative to assemble a team of people who know they are part of the crisis-management team should something pop up. It should include members of PR, social media, legal and even human resources, as they all have unique perspectives to any given situation. Each person should be equipped with each member's home and cell numbers. Though most PR people will tell you that their jobs never really end, other areas of the business may not be used to checking email and voicemail on the weekend. Well, if you're on the crisis team, you need to be on top of communications and not ignore your email. People need to be able to reach you. In addition, it's especially important for the person who manages social media to be very on top of the branded platforms. As I mentioned earlier, many a crisis is first discovered on social media.

11. Delivery of the apology is everything. One company once put its CEO on YouTube to issue a video apology for a comment he made that was entirely inappropriate. He was AWFUL. Not only was he terrible on camera, but he was also reading a teleprompter, which was obvious to anyone who watched. So if you have to put a public face on an apology, think about whom you have at your disposal who not only has the "right" title but is also capable of the task at hand.

Remember that constitutional right of freedom of speech? Well, technically we still have it, but there are most definitely repercussions for it. If you put it out there, you need to be really sure you can stand by your words. With the Oscars dress fiasco, I had a responsibility to tell the fans what really happened. You might ask yourself, "Why?" Well, I took them along a journey, and when you invite people into your world, you can't just leave them hanging. That's not transparent, and transparency is a cornerstone of social media. With Steve's scenario he never even contemplated that his words could be detrimental. He posted those tweets and never gave them another thought. Social media can amplify the voice of every single person, no matter how big the following. That's powerful, and with power comes responsibility.

PART IV

Creating the Brand of You

CHAPTER FIFTEEN

Being Your Own Publicist

I'LL NEVER FORGET WHEN I WAS AT *ATELIER MAGA-ZINE* AND I WOULD CALL IN HERMÈS BIRKIN BAGS FOR A SHOOT. THE SAMPLES WOULD ARRIVE WITH AN inventory sheet that would detail exactly what I borrowed. But then, the PR people at Hermès took it a step further. A warning read, "Please inspect this sample upon receiving. We loaned it to you in perfect condition. If it is returned to us with any scratches or marks, you will be charged for the replacement of the handbag." *Gulp.* Please note the package also included white cloth gloves to handle the sample. Pretentious for a simple leather bag? *Yes.* Did I believe the hype? *Yes.* We all drank the Hermès punch. I borrowed plenty of major designer bags for shoots—everyone from Chanel to Saint Laurent. No brand asked us to treat their bags in the way Hermès did. Hermès showed us that they valued their samples and in turn, so should we or we would pay...dearly.

Was there a legitimate reason they took their bags so seriously? They certainly wanted us to understand the artisan handwork behind each bag. I was even once invited to attend a Hermès sewing event, where I learned and experienced what went into making an Hermès design. It wasn't simple. It certainly was artisan. Was it involved? *Yes.* Was it worth the price they charge? *Probably not.* But they walked the walk. Hermès decided what value they wanted to hold in the minds of their consumer, and so it was. Yes, they have hundreds of years of heritage, and yes, it takes countless hours and artisans to make each style, but at the end of the day they made public perception exactly what they wanted it to be.

With that in mind, people can also decide what they want their public perception to be and they can actually shape it. Think about all the people you know and how you have labeled them: She's the stressed-out one. He's the lazy one. She is always so productive. He is an overachiever. I bet if you think about your top ten closest friends, you can sum each of them up in a one-sentence description. We're all innately judgmental even subconsciously. So the question is, how would your friends or colleagues describe you? And is that the message you want to convey? If it's not, you need to change it. You need to self-examine and decide what you want to stand for and what you want your personal brand to be.

Shaping a brand is indeed an art. Take, as another example, how a publicist manages a photo shoot at a celebrity client's home. They are next to the photographer at all times. They are directing what can and cannot be shot. They are curating the story and creating the point of view in the way they want their client perceived. Their strategy is one you can mimic, editing your life for public consumption in the same way. You need to think like a publicist, but as a publicist for YOURSELF. You are the brand.

But first, what is a brand? The American Marketing Association defines a brand as "A name, term, design, symbol or any other feature that identifies one seller's good or service as distinct from those of other sellers." A brand in many ways is an identity. Branding on a personal level is the art of aligning what you want people to think about you with what people *actually* think about you.

Personal branding for non-celebrities is a relatively new idea, even for me; I never thought about personal branding until it started coming up as a catchphrase in social media. Prior to that, the only people who were considered brands were celebrities. For the rest of us, the closest we got to a personal brand was our reputation. To be clear, caring about your reputation was always valuable. But what changed, thanks to social media, is your ability to strategically shape and amplify your personal brand's message. Publicists do this daily, so why not do it for yourself?

Most people wouldn't naturally think of themselves as a brand, but there are a lot of reasons you should. People are consuming your words, actions and how you present yourself in various ways. The sum of those ways is your identity. But is that the identity that you even want? I'm a firm believer that every person has something unique to offer and that branding yourself is the best way to make sure people know what that is.

To do this you need to look at yourself from an outsider's point of view. Forget the person you are. Step outside yourself and pretend for a moment that you are a public relations executive and your new client is YOU.

No matter the industry, a publicist's strategy for generating brand awareness is the same. A publicist always considers:

1. What are the best products or assets that I have to work with?

2. What's my hook or story? (a.k.a. What will the media, and ultimately the public, care about?)
3. How do I create an emotional connection between my product/brand and the audience it's intended for?
4. Where is the best place to launch this strategy? (Print, online, socially, etc.)

When crafting your personal brand, you need to keep those angles in mind while answering the following questions:

1. Who are you? What are the core principles that you stand for? You can think of these answers from both a professional and a personal standpoint. Write down three to five words that answer this question. The fewer words you can describe yourself in, the tighter your "filter" is.
2. What do you want to be known for? Every good brand gives off an air of expertise in a specific area. **INSIDER TIP: A lot of people do a lot of things, but the person who does it the loudest gets the "expert" credit.**
3. What are marketable qualities or talents that are unique to you? Do you promote them?
4. What do people remember most after meeting you? Consult with friends and colleagues who can give you honest feedback on this answer.

These are NOT easy questions, but I will show you how to navigate this thought process and come to a conclusion that you can digest and use to your benefit.

Step One: Get to know yourself by writing your bio. A bio is a summary of you, your professional and your personal lives. It's everything you are that you probably never thought to put on paper. Famous people have bios because if someone in the press is doing a story on them, it gives that reporter an easy, digestible snapshot of the celebrity's life and career. It is essentially a summary of your personal brand.

Bios are written in the third person, which is genius for the purposes of your branding exercise, because it allows you to take a step back and not feel totally awkward talking about yourself. So when you're writing your bio, pretend that you're a journalist who is writing an article about you for the New York Times. Instead of writing things like "I did," write "He [or she] did." It's an out-of-body experience, one that will help you understand who you are and what you have done so far. Also, it's OK to brag a little, so do list your most important accomplishments. But remember, a good journalist has a critical eye. If there are some less-than-stellar facts about you, it's important to include those. You need to paint a vivid picture of yourself—not just what you have done, but who you are as a person. What is your personality like? How do you present yourself? What do you look like? Throw it all in there.

Things to touch upon in your bio:

1. Personality/physical attributes
2. Education
3. Career path, important jobs and titles
4. Hobbies
5. Passions
6. Talents, awards, etc.
7. Marital/family status
8. Affiliations, charity or otherwise

Write your bio in chronological order: Start with your current position and then take people through a brief synopsis of the past. Include only the most noteworthy points, the things that really have had an impact on who you are today. The goal of the bio is to show how you got where you are. If you can try to keep it under five hundred words, you will challenge yourself to be edited. When you start writing, you might get to a place where you have nothing left to say. That's OK, because your story is never actually done. Life is to-be-continued, right?

Once you reach that stopping point, cozy up in a chair somewhere and pretend that you're reading a story about someone else. Do you like this person? Are you impressed by what he's done? What do you feel this person should change about himself? Be objective. Pretend it's not you that you're reading about.

So what do you think? Did you paint an accurate picture of yourself? Were you being honest? If someone Googled you, would they be able to write the same story based on what came up about you in their search results? Are there pictures, if not articles, that come up in the search that tell your story? Is that the story you want told? Would you write it in your *New York Times* article?

You have to ask yourself these questions so you can get a real assessment of what you're dealing with. Do you need to start doing more of something? Do you need to start doing less?

Step Two: Make your life "word cloud" by pulling out the keywords in your bio that really summarize your story. These words will essentially describe the overall picture in a list format. The stronger the attribute, the bigger the word should appear.

Step Three: Find an image for each word that you pulled out and create a mood board of your life. Take a step back. What does it look like altogether? What do you want to keep? What do you want to change?

Step Four: Continue the journey. Since your story will end right in the middle somewhere, think about where you want it to go. Start imagining what you want the rest of the article to say. Continue writing it all out *as if* it has already happened, but this time in *italics*—all your aspirations, everything you want to accomplish. Perfect the story until it reads exactly the way you would want it to be printed in the *New York Times*.

This all may sound like a lot of work and a lot of soul-searching—and it is. But, when you're finished, you will know yourself so much better. Your article might be tough to read and you might not like it, but that's OK. This could be the match that lights the fire under you to make some positive changes.

People don't innately like to look at themselves in the same way that most actors don't like to watch themselves on camera. But to improve in any area, you need to be honest with yourself about who you are, where you are and where you are heading. How do you connect with people in your world? Do they feel you have something special to offer? Do they get value from knowing you? If the answer is yes, it's that value you uniquely offer those around you that you need to promote and capitalize on.

But I want to be very clear about something: **Personal branding is not about becoming famous.** In fact, that's the least it's about. Personal branding is about **self-reflection and ultimately outward presentation. Personal branding is about identifying the best version of you and striving**

toward achieving and communicating that every day. If you think like a publicist, you will be conscious about how others perceive your message and you will be able to fix that perception as needed. Being conscious of your personal brand will allow you to perform better in every area of your life, no matter what you do.

Every day gives you an opportunity to reimagine yourself differently. If you are brave enough to really look at yourself with eyes wide open, you will be all the better for it. There is no right answer here. The closest you will get is being happy and proud in your own skin and to me, that's worth a hell of a lot. What you do with your personal brand depends on you. How hard do you want to work on it and how committed are you to shaping it? The answer had better be "very," because no one is going to do the work for you. You are your best PR person.

CHAPTER SIXTEEN

Casting Yourself in a New Leading Role

AFTER YOU'VE READ YOUR BIO, YOU SHOULD HAVE A CLEAR PICTURE OF WHO YOU ARE AND HOPEFULLY WHAT YOU WANT YOUR PERSONAL BRAND TO STAND for. The way people perceive you goes beyond what you say and how you work with others. What about your image? Does it match your personal brand? Image is a powerful asset; it's the thing people consume before you have even opened your mouth.

Have you ever walked down the street and seen someone and thought, "That looks like *somebody*." I don't mean someone you know or someone famous; I mean a person who gives off an air of importance. Maybe it was the way she held her head high or her killer outfit, or maybe it was the way he walked with purpose. Perhaps it was the whole package. But something made you take notice and in an instant, an impression was made.

Confidence speaks volumes. How we present ourselves affects people's perceptions of us. What people see and feel when they meet us is how they judge us. I know that hurts, but the whole "don't judge a book by its cover" thing is total bullshit. People will judge anything *before* they actually know what someone or something really has to offer. You want proof? Tell me you didn't judge the very cover of this book before you bought it? I know you did. We all judge books by their covers—at least initially.

So given that everyone does it, why not use that information strategically? Your image matters and you have the power to change it. How you currently present yourself is not your only option. In fact, you can change mostly anything you want to. Actors do it all the time. They examine the role they need to play. They study the personality, the look and the attitude. They are clear about what they need to do to become that character. There's no reason that it can't work the same way in real life. You can reshape your image over and over again.

People who have poise and presence feel more important than people who don't. That's just how it is. If you walk into a room like you own it, people will believe that you do. Now I'm not advising you to be a bulldozer. As I've already mentioned in this book, there's a big difference between confident and cocky. I'm saying that the key is to be comfortable in your own skin and believe that you have something to offer, because YOU DO.

The most important question you can ask yourself is "What impression do I make on the people who meet me?" The reality is that people do not have that much imagination when it comes to other people. What you show them is the only thing they will know. If you're really shy, for example, no one is going to imagine you getting up in front of a large audience or even a room full of executives and giving a great presentation. If you want people to imagine you in certain roles, you have to help them see you that way. If you want to be asked to give that presentation, make sure people know you have a voice. And even if you're truly uncomfortable having a voice, it's OK to force yourself through it.

There are many tools that you can employ to help you convey a certain image. Style is one of them. Style is a visual extension of your personality. In any business, fashion can help define your image. Don't believe me? Imagine you were hiring a lawyer and he walked in wearing a suit one size too small that looked like it hadn't been dry-cleaned in months. Would you ignore your impression of him? Or would you start to doubt his qualifications? I'm betting it would be the latter.

Think back to your bio. Do you currently project the right image for the personal brand you want to build? Does your current look work for you or against you? Do you even have a look? It's true that there are certain professions where style perhaps does not factor in, but it matters in almost any profession I can think of. Great style naturally equates to confidence.

The first step is establishing a "look" that is purely you. If you choose a look and stick with it, it will become memorable to others. **INSIDER TIP: Repetition IS reputation!**

My "thing" has always been being dressed up. I can't help it; I just feel better that way. In college, when everyone was rolling out of bed in their sweatpants from the night before, I was decked in a head-to-toe outfit. I wouldn't dream of wearing sweatpants. Being properly dressed in pants, a skirt or even a dress affected my mood and changed my mind-set. I actually believed that being dressed up allowed me to pay more attention in class. Even at nineteen, I knew my A game had something to do with fashion.

I'm still the same way. People are always surprised when they see me in casual clothes (which is limited to the weekends). Then there's my signature red lipstick. I blame my sister Ilana for this one, because even at two years old, she would not let our mother leave the house without wearing bright lipstick. She would literally say, "Mommy, lips, lips." In turn, when I started wearing makeup, I naturally gravitated to a bright lip. (In truth, I look dead without it). Red lipstick is my signature color now and I would feel funny if I ever wore another. I also only wear red nail polish because my pale skin looks better with a bright contrast. The truth is, people lock in their "signature" look because that is what naturally looks best on them or makes them feel the best.

I'll admit it: I'm old-school. I was raised to believe that you should go out feeling good about yourself. I've never regretted taking that extra primp time, especially when I inevitably run into the person I least want to see. Murphy's Law! Taking pride in your look gives off a specific impression; it shows the world that you value yourself. Like the great Diana Vreeland once said, "I loathe narcissism, but I approve of vanity."

So the question is, what image do you want to portray? You can find a look that's right for you—or better yet, find a look that matches what you want to do. That old saying "dressing for the job you want, not the job you have" still has a lot of merit.

Celebrity stylists play this "what image do you want to portray?" game every day with their clients. As I am privy to the strategic decisions many stylists make when shaping their client's image, I can tell you that it is all totally thought out, every detail.

When I first learned about what really goes into shaping

a celebrity's style image, I was actually surprised by how simple it was to change perception. You know the drill; take a trashy-styled celeb and put her in an Oscar de la Renta full-skirted, tea-length frock and all of a sudden she gets newfound fashion cred.

A great example of how style transformation happens occurred one day when I had a very open conversation about strategy with a stylist friend. The conversation went down like this:

"We're going in a totally different direction with CelebX, I promise," Jake said. "Her publicist wants her fresh. You know, that all-American girl. That's why we're not putting her in European designers anymore. She's the chic girl next door. We want her relatable."

"OK, Jake," I said. "I'll consider giving you something from the new collection, but I need a promise from you that she will only wear us to the first premiere, not some random city."

"Done and done," Jake said. And just like that, CelebX's new style image was born.

But this strategic thinking is not just for celebrities. The right look can transform you. Clothes certainly do not make a person, but good ones sure do help.

Just imagine for a moment having a stylist whose job it is to worry about you: how you look and what you wear. Life would be easy, right? Well, think again. Even with a brilliant stylist, choosing the right look for the image a celebrity wants to portray is not always seamless.

Cue the flashback TV waves. It was Golden Globes season. As a fashion publicist, if you miss an opportunity to dress someone for the Golden Globes, it's horrendous because between TV and film, there are soooo many people going. But the designer competition is still fierce, not only because there are so many gowns to choose from, but also because there are a ton of celebrities who have existing relationships with brands or designers—whether it is that they are a good "friend of the house" or they are the face of the brand's ad campaign. Plus a brand is not open to dressing everyone; some celebs may be "off brand," a.k.a. not right for the brand's image. It's a crapshoot, really.

One year, we had this amazing bordeaux gown, one that I felt in my gut had a real chance of gracing the red carpet. Gowns are our awards-season currency. That season, the bordeaux gown was our breadwinner.

Cassandra, a great celebrity stylist, had been to our office as soon as the nominations had come out to see what we were cooking up for awards season. There are a lot of stylists who work in fashion and Hollywood. Some are good and some are not. Cassandra was a keeper. She treated the clothes with the love and affection they deserved. Sadly, that's not always the case. I've seen poorly trained assistants toss $25,000 gowns like balled-up paper napkins into the bottom of a trunk. I've seen beaded gowns come back crushed and covered in body makeup and deodorant. It's not pretty. Hey, I get upset if I see the clip of a hanger denting satin, so just know that I'm extra sensitive. I mostly get upset because I know how much love and effort these designers, patternmakers and sewers put into every garment. It's an art, and when you have to work with some people who just don't get it, it's painful. A great stylist knows the design process and reveres it. Cassandra was one of those stylists.

Cassandra was dressing several clients that season,

including a young, gorgeous actress who I will call Jenny who had just starred in a major movie. Even though she wasn't a nominee, this was Jenny's breakout role. I was confident that her presence on the carpet would be huge. I had never worked with Jenny before, but I loved Cassandra. She was great to work with, and most importantly, she had the trust and faith of her clients.

Cassandra worked with us to make sure the gown was remade perfectly to Jenny's measurements. (Of course, Jenny was bound to drop five pounds right before Globes day anyway, so we always hedged on the smaller size.)

I was so happy with the way this gown was turning out; it was sure to be a success on Golden Globes night. Of course, we didn't put all our eggs in one basket, as we did have other gowns out with other celebrities in LA, but none quite as good. In my heart, I was counting on Jenny to work out. I needed her to.

Cassandra was great at keeping me abreast of our status after each fitting. There are usually two to three fittings and alterations per gown. Making it through these rounds is huge and spirit-lifting. I will inevitably hold my breath or pace back and forth each time, waiting for *the* phone call. Did we make it? Or did we get edited out? Fate is in another's hands. If you are lucky enough to confirm an A-lister in your gown on awards night, it is one of the most satisfying feelings ever.

You would think that by the Saturday of the Globes, the dress would be decided and put to bed. Shockingly, a lot still happens that day as most celebs are still hemming and hawing over their choices. If the bordeaux gown was the first choice, believe me, there was a backup gown hanging in that room. The worst part about the backup gown is that the designer of that gown never knows it's the backup. "Oh you're one of two!" they tell you. Yeah, that's 50 percent. If I got a fifty on an exam, my parents would have had my head. I knew that our gown had made a trip to Lorraine Schwartz (the jeweler), which is always a great sign. The honor of having jewelry pulled to match your gown means they're considering the gown very seriously.

Jenny was going to fit at six p.m. LA time on Saturday. It was just a quick "let's see it one more time" non-fitting. Cassandra was so excited about the gown, too. She was really feeling it, Jenny was feeling it and that was a great thing, because all our other gowns had failed out by then. Another bonus was that Jenny was asked to present, which meant she would be onstage. More airtime! More press! Yay! We rock!

I was at dinner when Jenny's fitting started, constantly checking my phone for a text from Cassandra. By eleven p.m. New York time, I had heard nothing. Now, a normal fitting can take hours—some even last all day, depending on how many gowns there are. But this was not really a fitting, this was a "let's just try it one more time" fitting. By one a.m. I decided to text Cassandra:

Today 1:00 AM

Hello? Is everything ok? —Aliza

Today 1:15 AM

Sorry to be MIA. Fitting went great, will call you tomorrow. —C

PHEW!! I couldn't breathe there for a while. I fell asleep at two a.m. peacefully.

By eight a.m. on Globes Sunday I woke up like someone

had blown a whistle in my ear. Any texts? No. Any voice-mails? No. Emails? No. All was quiet on the West Coast front. It's hard to do anything else on an awards show Sunday except stare at my devices scouring for information. I had no reason to be nervous, though. Jenny's fitting the night before went "great." Cassandra said so. Well, she didn't use an exclamation point, now that I was thinking about it. She said "great," and a comma was not as happy as an exclamation point. I started freaking out about any clues I could find hidden in her punctuation and tone. I stayed home all day, checking the time in every room I went into. The red carpet begins at six p.m. EST, so that means three p.m. in LA, which means by eleven a.m. or so, celebrities are starting to get into hair and makeup depending on what they need done (like hair extensions or a quickie dye job, for example).

At noon I considered texting Cassandra just to check in, but then decided against it. If there was a problem, she would call me. No news was good news. I'm sure Cassandra was busy steaming the gown and making sure that the jewelry and accessories were all laid out for Jenny so when she went over to get her dressed, everything was organized.

In LA, that's exactly what was happening. Jenny's house was buzzing with all her peeps—manager, publicist, stylist, hairdresser, makeup artist, manicurist, and Jenny's sister was over, too.

At one p.m., Cassandra texted me:

Today 1:00 PM

Getting dressed! —C

Today 1:02 PM

AHHH! So excited! Can't wait to see her! —A

Today 1:28 PM

Call me. —C

I stopped dead in my tracks. Staring at my phone, it was as if "Call me" was pulsing. Dread started to wash over me. As I picked up the phone, I started to panic. My heart was racing and I just knew something was wrong.

"Cassandra? It's Aliza."

"Aliza," Cassandra said in a whisper. "I'm in the bathroom. I am so, so sorry but Jenny's sister came over to help her get dressed and she just told her that she thinks the gown is stunning, but since Jenny isn't nominated, she thinks it's too much. She told her she looks like she's trying too hard."

WHAAAAT? My eyes started to well up. I couldn't even get the words out. I was completely paralyzed.

"Aliza? Can you hear me? I'm sorry I have to whisper; they are in the other room," Cassandra said.

"I heard you, Cassandra. I just can't believe she is going to let her sister's one comment completely wipe out what she has wanted this whole time."

"I know, I agree one hundred percent, Aliza, but there is nothing I can do. Her mind is made up. It's really important for her to nail this; she wants people to respect her. I'm so, so sorry. I know how hard you worked for this, how hard we all did. I will make it up to you."

"Thank you, Cassandra, I have to go," I said, half swallowing my voice. I hung up the phone, devastated. We had no one. Jenny's sister had ultimately made the decision, trumping her brilliant stylist, publicist and manager. Her sister's perception was Jenny's reality. That bordeaux gown told too much of a story, made her too important, and that importance should be saved for when she's really nominated. Her personal brand was not ready for a big-league gown. She had to get to first base first, and that called for something a little more "presenter" level and a lot less "nominee." How's that for an ego pop? I was crushed, but the real victim here was Jenny. The last person who entered the room was controlling her image and wasn't even trained to do so.

Now clearly this is not the case with every celebrity. In fact, some of them don't even employ stylists and do a fabulous job by themselves. But for the ones who do, I wish that they would just let their stylist do what they are paid to do. My favorite stylists are the ones who hold the most power over a look. After all, they are paid to know what's best for that client.

A great stylist would be the first to tell you that finding the image that works best for your personal brand isn't easy and often takes trial and error. But the point is that it can be reimagined over and over again. You can cast yourself in a new leading role with the right style direction. There's nothing wrong with relying on your friends or family to be your sounding board, but just remember that you have to be comfortable and happy with the image you are portraying from start to finish. After all, you can't wear high heels if you don't know how to walk in them, and let's be honest, nothing is worse than a girl who wobbles.

MUST DO: FIND AND KEEP YOUR PERSONAL STYLE

1. Know thy body! One size does not fit all. Certain styles look better for your shape than others. Don't convince yourself that you should be able to wear everything, because you're doing yourself a disservice.

2. Get style-inspired: Gather images of people whose style you most admire. Make a mood board of those people. I bet they will all have a lot of things in common. For example, if you end up choosing ten women who are all wearing tailored clothing—proper jackets and pants—then you obviously want to give off a more sophisticated, professional impression. Try to find the common denominators in the pictures. If you had to put their style in a sentence, what would that sentence be?

3. Record best outfits: Believe it or not, a good style moment can be forgotten in a nanosecond. If you find a great look that made you feel wonderful that day, write it down, or better yet photograph it. Trust me, your brain won't remember it otherwise.

4. Hang by look: If you're not an organized person, please skip to number five. If you are, consider hanging some of your important looks together. It helps immensely, especially if you don't record or photograph the look as I recommended in step three.

5. Identify your go-to clothes and store them together: Your go-to clothes are the pieces that never let you down. They are, for example, the pants that fit no matter what you ate that week. Or the shirt that never wrinkles even though you have forgotten to dry-clean it for months. Knowing what your go-to pieces are will save you when you are pressed

for time or having a moment where nothing is working and you have a big meeting!

6. Keep your job in mind: No matter how much fun you want to have with your personal style, you still need to remember the job you have. Your style needs to match your profession. Sorry, was that news? You don't want expressing yourself to make a negative impact.

7. Invest in key items: If you do nothing else, invest in the pieces that people remember most, like shoes, handbags and coats.

8. Stay in your comfort zone: You don't want clothing to ever look like a costume, and if you're wearing something that you don't feel comfortable in, people know.

9. Identify a signature item: As I have said previously, repetition is reputation. If you repeat something over and over again, people will associate that item with you. For me, it's the red lipstick and red nails, but it could be a piece of clothing, jewelry, a hairstyle, anything really.

Style is one factor in creating your personal brand, and it's probably the easiest way to reinvent yourself; it's also the most creative. You may be thinking to yourself that style doesn't matter for what you do or want to do, but I promise you that having a strong sense of personal style leads to confidence in other more important areas.

Just remember though, no matter what happens on the outside, it's always going to be the inside that matters. How do you feel? Your style needs to empower you to take on the world each day. That's what fashion does for me. It gives me the energy and confidence to tackle whatever comes my way. Well, that and coffee.

CHAPTER SEVENTEEN

When You Get to the Top, Don't Be an Asshole

IN SECOND GRADE I DECIDED TO BE A TEACHER. NO, *REALLY*. I ACTUALLY GATHERED THREE OF MY FRIENDS AND TOLD THEM THAT I WAS GOING TO BE THEIR teacher and assign them homework each evening. I called it the Homework Club. How original! (*S) Every day I would come up with a lesson and they would take it home, do it and hand it in the next day. I would grade their work with Hello Kitty stickers.

People always seem to put greater importance on being a leader, but the ironic thing is that being a follower is just as essential. Remember, you can't have one without the other. Some people are born to lead and others are meant to follow. At different times in your life you might shift from one role to the other. However, if you take on a leadership role it's imperative that you understand how to do it well. A good leader is motivating to her team and doesn't feel above them. She would throw herself in the trenches and work just as hard as anyone else. She compliments a job well done and is constructive about mistakes made. She gives credit where credit is due, and she lets her team shine when they deserve to.

Take a Selfie: Do You Know How to Lead a Team?

1. Do people respect you? Because if they don't, you need to work on earning that respect, first and foremost.
2. Are you a motivating leader? Do you have the ability to get people energized about a project?
3. Do you have a clear vision about what needs to be done and how you and your team are going to accomplish it?
4. Have you researched anything that might be happening at the same time as your project? Personal commitments can get in the way of a perfect plan. So carve out the time you need in advance.
5. Have you conveyed a clear message? Don't assume that people understand the project—if you are managing a team, you need to make sure they see the bigger picture so they understand the full scope of what you're trying to do.
6. Are you a good manager? Group emails never work. If you're leading a team you must follow up with each person individually to keep them on point. Micromanage if you think you must! People might not like it, but a "gentle" reminder of deadlines can actually save people from making huge mistakes.

> Note: People confuse micromanaging for condescension, and it is not. If you don't like to be micromanaged, then shoot your supervisor a quick email to let her know that things have been taken care of. I love nothing more than when someone responds to an email with "done."

7. Remember the meaning of assume? Don't assume anything is being done until you confirm it. Miscommunication happens every day and it can be extremely costly.

8. Are you appreciative of your team's efforts? Remember to thank anyone who has helped you make your project a success. Nothing is worse than killing yourself for a boss to get something done and then when it is finally finished and executed flawlessly, all you hear are pin drops.

Patti Cohen has been leading the communications strategy at Donna Karan International since the creation of the company. She is my boss and mentor. Of course, when I was starting out at the company, I didn't have the luxury of reporting to her. I only started reporting to her when I become an executive some years ago. Patti's exemplary leadership is known in the fashion industry at large. She is an icon, and her reputation for being one of the loveliest, most genuine people in fashion precedes her wherever she goes. Patti is always the leader, but she is a generous one. She is not afraid to let her team shine. She hasn't just allowed my growth at Donna Karan International, she has created it. She is most definitely the singular reason I have never left. Of course I love the brand, but the people matter so much more. I credit Patti for helping me be the boss and mentor I have become today, and I am forever grateful for her wisdom, support and generosity of spirit.

When you see someone really powerful be gracious and supportive, you can't help but be impressed. You also can't help but think, "Why can't everyone be like that?" And why would people do a good job for you if you're not? Sure, you may get the results that you want a few times, but ultimately your team will stop working for you because they won't want you to succeed. Well, you can't be successful without a great team. The ability to motivate and influence others is essential.

Before Patti, I was fortunate to have Elizabeth, another generous boss who encouraged me to grow. But here's a funny postscript to that story. When I started writing this book, I called Elizabeth to reminisce and fill in some of the blanks in my memory about my time at *Atelier Magazine*. She remembered a lot of the same things I did, but one thing she enlightened me on was my interview with Heather. Are you sitting down? Because this was certainly breaking news to me—my interview with Heather didn't go as well as I thought. Essentially, when I left the office after meeting with her, she'd called Elizabeth in and said, "Are you sure you want to hire 'THAT' girl?" (When Elizabeth told me this, my jaw dropped to the floor.) Heather had proceeded to say, "You don't think she's too aggressive? That you won't end up working for HER?" Ouch. I was twenty-two years old and I can promise you that I was not aggressive. In fact, Elizabeth agreed. What I was, however, was confident.

When you know that you will do anything to get the job done, that gives you confidence. When people appreciate your work, like Dean and the team at *Haute Magazine* did, that makes you confident. Heather was a different breed though, and I'd bet my life that when she was trying to rise through the ranks, there were a lot of people who tried to keep her down. Just a guess, but I bet a very good one. Since I was literally nowhere on the totem pole, she didn't think I had the right to be confident.

At the time of my interview, Elizabeth explained to Heather that she loved my personality and energy and, no, she was not scared that she would end up working for me. Learning this so many years later was a complete shock to my system. It took me a few minutes to really comprehend the reality of this conversation. Did I almost not get that job? That's the truth, right? Lucky for me, Elizabeth was very confident in herself and definitive. Her opinion of me weighed heavily in the decision. In a nutshell, if it weren't for Elizabeth, my career in fashion could have stopped short right there.

I would like to take a moment here to talk about strong people supporting strong people. As someone who's now in a position to hire people, I can tell you many a candidate has come into my office for an interview and completely scared the pants off my team. Their issue is always "she's too much" or "he's too in-your-face." Everyone seems to be put off by people who know what they want and who believe they can be an asset to the team. I sit in a different chair because I know that I was once that girl. If I had intimidated Elizabeth, I might not be telling you this story right now. With that said, it bears repeating that there is a big difference between confident and cocky.

It's imperative that we support and celebrate others who have a great sense of self. Exclusively surrounding oneself with small people might make someone feel big, but it's a false sense of strength. The stronger the team you build underneath yourself, the more you can accomplish.

INSIDER TIP: Real leaders are never afraid of the people who walk behind them. Real leaders are too busy looking ahead to the future to care.

Leadership is a combination of pushing and pulling. You have to strike a balance between giving orders and being one of the team. I've always found that the key to leading is not only having the skills to lead but also being a likeable leader.

Take a Selfie: Are You a Likeable Leader?

1. Do you give credit where credit is due? There is nothing more deflating than having someone take credit for someone else's work. Don't do it! There's also nothing more unlikeable than a person who claims to know and do everything. Spread the wealth.

2. Do you compliment your team members? A compliment is free of charge, and giving one will make you feel as good as the person who receives it.

3. Do you show your human side? Sure you're the boss, but that doesn't mean that you have to act like a robot. A likeable leader shows she cares about her team.

4. Do you leverage talent? So what if your assistant just started; if she's good at x, y and z, why not let her add that to her plate? Employees want to know that they are being recognized for the skills they have. If you show an employee that you recognize her strengths and continue to grow her, she will stay. Keeping your team intact and promoting from within is the sign of a strong manager. Companies like strong managers.

5. Are you honest? Your team will know if you're not and they will start to distrust you. Openness and transparency are not only appreciated, they are required. Without honesty there is no respect.
6. Have you been back to the trenches? Showing your team that you are willing to pitch in goes a long way.
7. Are you fair? You need to keep your team motivated, so don't pick favorites.
8. Are you able to solve conflicts amicably?
9. Are you open to new ideas?
10. Are you confusing likeability with being a yes-man? Don't. Leaders still need to be assertive and decisive.

Over the years, I have made it my business to try to shepherd good candidates, like Dean and Elizabeth (and of course Patti in my later career) did for me. When you help someone achieve something greater than they could have achieved alone, that's powerful. People don't always realize that the more people you help, the bigger the network you ultimately build for yourself. That means you have more people to call upon when it's your turn to need help. **INSIDER TIP: Good karma is actually good business.**

But the best leaders are in touch with who they are. They are aware of their faults and are constantly self-assessing their management style. They are collaborative and open to change. A leader is only as good as the people who follow. So as you rise through the ranks, remember the endgame. It's not about the corner office, it's about being able to motivate and inspire others. The better you get at leading a group, the more all of you will accomplish.

CHAPTER EIGHTEEN

Making Cocktails Count

I HAD BEEN INTERNING AT *HAUTE MAGAZINE* A FEW MONTHS WHEN DEAN, BEING THE AMAZING BOSS HE WAS, INVITED ME TO ATTEND A FASHION EVENT with him. It was a cocktail party to celebrate a new shoe collection. I was so proud to have been invited, and while I never would've thought for a moment that my role was anything beyond "lucky intern," it still felt great to at least appear like I belonged.

At the event, I was standing with Dean having a glass of champagne, when all of a sudden a woman came running over to greet him. "Dean dahling!!!!!!! It's wonderful to see you!" she exclaimed with a double air-kiss and a thick Italian accent.

He returned the greeting, then said, "Monica, I would like you to meet…"

Before he even had a chance to introduce me, Monica (who, it turned out, was the wife of the designer) jumped in with, "Oh my god, I have not seen you in forever! How are you, my darling? It's so good to see you!"

Wait, was she talking to me?? There was no way she

could have known me. I was nobody! A lowly intern! I started to panic, with visions of her gushing about people she thought we had in common but I likely didn't know. So I decided to politely correct her.

"Monica, I'm so sorry, but I think you have me mistaken for someone else. You see, I'm Dean's intern."

Well, she did not like being corrected and she basically huffed and stormed off. As I died inside, I turned to Dean and profusely apologized for embarrassing his friend and, subsequently, him. Sure, I could have played along with Monica, but she had caught me off guard and I was scared she'd end up catching me in a lie. But Dean thought the whole thing was hilarious and so—phew!—I got lucky my first time out.

Hindsight is twenty-twenty. Today before I attend any event, I always take a few moments to Google all the possible important players expected to be in attendance. You can't go to a party where you don't know what the host looks like, and while you're at it, you may as well also know her left- and right-hand people. With the Internet, there's really no excuse not to be completely proficient in key faces and names. This is totally a PR thing to do, but I think it applies to any industry. Knowledge is power, but knowledge also means not embarrassing yourself by not knowing who people are.

But even when you know the man of the hour, you can still learn new ways to improve your IRL social game. A few years ago, I had the distinct pleasure of attending a private cocktail party in the home of my husband's boss, hosted by none other than President Bill Clinton. And since it was a small gathering, all of us there knew we'd have a chance to meet him.

President Clinton is widely known to have a charismatic personality, but I didn't quite understand to what extent, until I spoke to him. He was as charming and mesmerizing as everyone says he is. He made all of us feel like he was genuinely interested in what we had to say and who we were. I'm entirely sure he forgot about us all a second later, but that didn't really matter. What mattered is how special he made us all feel in that moment.

I remember my mother telling me when I was little, "Make sure you look people in the eye," but this was on another level. I went home that night thinking about how I behave when people speak to me. Am I really listening? Do I really care? Even if I don't care, do I show that I do? It was a really interesting test to give myself, so I decided that from that day on, I would take a cue from the president and make a concerted effort to really listen to other people, to make them feel heard.

A wise man once said, "You can't be interesting unless you're interested." Because people like to talk and want to be heard, those who truly listen play a valuable role in the social food chain. I decided to pay attention to the roles people play at cocktail parties, where there are usually lots of quick conversations as you bump into people you haven't seen in a while or get to know new people.

I conducted **The Cocktail Party Experiment** every time I went to a party—and shockingly, the same exact thing happened every single time. I would start off asking the other person how he was doing, and he'd of course happily answer. Then he'd go on and on and on and on about his job, all his recent accomplishments, blah, blah, blah. I would stand there thinking how completely self-absorbed this person was and how I was quite literally not speaking.

After carrying on for a few conceited minutes, the other person would catch himself, as if to think, "Oops, I haven't asked her about herself!" Then he'd say, "Enough about me! How are you???"

That was my cue. "I'm fine, everything is pretty much the same, all good," I would say. He would then ask a specific question, and when I would begin to answer, he would cut me off and flip the conversation back around to him. It was truly amazing. By doing so, he showed me that he really didn't give a damn about how I was or what I had to say. He was way more interested in talking about himself. (And though I may have used a hypothetical "he" in this scenario, rest assured the same thing happened when I chatted with women.)

I would love to tell you that this scenario was limited to just one particular person, but sadly that was not the case. As I kept conducting this experiment, I was always the interested one, the one who held the gaze and listened to every word the other person had to say. It saddened and amazed me at the same time. On the bright side though, maybe that made me the most desirable person in the room to talk to. Hey, if it works for President Clinton...

Take a Selfie: Do You Know How to Cocktail Party?

One of the most important skills a person can learn is how to network. However, taking that a step further, you should learn and get comfortable with the idea of networking ALONE.

Here's a good test. You're invited to a cocktail party by a client. You don't have anyone to go with and you don't know anyone who'll be at the party except the client, who you know will be busy mingling with his guests. Do you go? Can you walk into that event alone and have a good time? A lot of people would rather die than go to an event alone. They just can't wrap their heads around going solo. But someone who knows they have something to offer has no problem going anywhere alone. You have to know your self-worth and be able to contribute to any conversation. A great way to test yourself is to go to an event that isn't related to your business. There's less pressure when you don't know anyone and you can take your cocktail party skills out for a spin.

The key to success here is to always remember that people love to talk about themselves, so the best way to start a conversation (especially with someone you don't know) is either to ask a question or throw out a compliment. Alternatively, if you know this person is going to be at the event, why not be prepared for what you are going to say? You could compliment something she recently did, like some sort of project or industry achievement. Another option is to choose the "we're in the same boat" route and talk about something you're both experiencing in that moment—for example, if you're at a bar and it's too crowded or the line to get a drink is long. The key is to find a common ground, something that the other person can relate to.

But your delivery is key. You need to play it cool and sound natural. Always think of yourself as equal to the person you're speaking with, even when that might not be the case. It will give you the confidence necessary to engage in a great conversation.

MUST DO: COCKTAIL PARTY CONVERSATION TIPS

1. Host 411: Know who your host is. It takes away any potential awkwardness and also makes you look really in the know. If you're going to a work-related event and you don't know the host personally, Google her. Know what she looks like. Know her title and have a bit of intel on some of her recent accomplishments.

2. Get Your Head Out of the Sand: If you know you'll be mingling with people later, read the news that day—not just news specific to your business, but news of the world. Nothing is worse than being in a group where everyone's talking about something major and you're standing there silent because you have no clue what happened. Being armed with this information will never go to waste, because you can always play the role of educator for the rest of the group, which comes with the added bonus of showing how well-read you are.

3. Push and Pull: The best conversations are ones where the roles shift. You give some spotlight, you take some spotlight. Be conscious of how much airtime you've had and graciously turn the tables back around to the other person. Ask questions that show you're really interested in what that person has to say. If he or she doesn't return the favor, just remember President Clinton and enjoy knowing you were the most engaged listener at the party and the person others remember as being so nice to talk to. It works like a charm.

4. Take a Breather: There is no point in hanging around talking to no one. Take a bathroom break, gather yourself and walk back in refreshed. Your phone is a great wingman, but just remember that people don't start talking to people who are on their phone. When you are in the room, you want to show that you are accessible.

5. Make Networking Work: If you make a connection at a party, get that person's business card. You never know where that connection will lead or when you might need to use it. BUT you must email that person the next day while you are fresh in his mind. Keep it short and simple. Something like:

> John,
>
> It was great to connect with you last night! Here's my info should you ever need it.
>
> Aliza

(Your email should have an automatic signature, complete with your name, title, company, etc.)

If the person you met is senior compared to you, it's always good to be a little more formal:

> Dear John,
>
> It was nice to meet you last night. I really enjoyed our conversation about _____. Have a great rest of your week.
>
> Best,
> Aliza Licht

(Your email should have an automatic signature, complete with your name, title, company, etc.)

A few things to note here:

1. I added "Dear" to the more formal email.
2. Reminding the person about something specific you discussed will hopefully spark his memory as to who you are.
3. It's presumptuous to think that this more senior person will ever need your contact info, so no need to point it out.
4. Watch your exclamation points. Exclamation points tend to make your tone more enthusiastic and also more casual. Use them sparingly if you're trying to come across as more professional.

What if the social gathering you're going to is with your coworkers, like an office-wide happy hour? Then there's no need to send follow-up emails to the people you talk to, obviously, but your professional cocktail etiquette still needs to be on point.

Let me be very clear. Just because you're invited to a work-related social gathering doesn't mean it's cool to throw back four cocktails and act like a blithering idiot. On the contrary, you should skip the alcohol altogether if you're someone who a) can't control your liquor or b) gets a loose tongue when you drink. Work events are a time to build and expand your network. I promise you that even when people are years into their careers, those who get wasted at the office Christmas party are not only judged, their behavior is never forgotten.

So, what do you talk about and how do you act?

1. Try not to talk about work-related projects or issues. People are out trying to forget about the daily grind. Don't be the office buzzkill.

2. Don't get roped into office gossip. If people are bashing a colleague behind her back, stay silent. Better yet, excuse yourself from the group by asking if anyone needs a drink.
3. Don't expect to hang with your boss. People are weird about hierarchy at work/social events. It's one thing if it happens naturally, but otherwise try to mingle with your peers.

Honing these skills will up your networking game immensely, but it's just as important to nurture relationships outside the office. Let's face it, knowing only one type of person is boring. I know some people in fashion who pretty much only hang out with people in fashion; same goes for some that I know in finance who only hang out with finance people. That's not going to make you well-rounded, and it's certainly not going to help you build your network. You also can't learn from people who know exactly the same things as you. I actually love meeting PR people who work in industries totally unrelated to fashion. They come at the profession from a totally different perspective, but the principles are the same.

Whether you do it through business groups, social events or even recreational sports, exposing yourself to a greater network outside your immediate circle will lead to unique opportunities to "cross-pollinate"—which not only gives you more resources to draw from, but also makes you a key connector between people. In fact, being that go-to person people call whenever they need a contact or an "in" will really establish your status, and ultimately your personal brand.

No matter how or where you choose to network, remember this: The most successful people are generous in spirit and happy to make an introduction for someone else even though it has no visible benefit to them. They're called uber-connectors. Being an uber-connector is good business karma and will only help you establish yourself as someone in the know.

But before you go out and network, make sure you are clear about what your personal brand stands for. You not only need to network for your job, you also need to network for yourself. Networking gives you an opportunity to leverage and communicate your personal brand while learning about another's. That exchange of information is mutually beneficial. **INSIDER TIP: If you don't know the message you are trying to convey, you won't be getting the most out of the experience.** If you think of each relationship that you build as a step on a ladder, the last one leads you to the next. If you keep on building those steps, you never know where you could end up.

CHAPTER NINETEEN

Presenting Like a Pro

MY EXPERIMENT IN BEING THE GOOD LISTENER AT PAR-
TIES NOTWITHSTANDING, I REALLY HAPPEN TO LOVE
PUBLIC SPEAKING. IN MAY 2013, I WAS ASKED TO BE
a keynote speaker at the first-ever TEDx Times Square conference in New York City. The mission of the TED conference is to proliferate "ideas worth spreading." My job was
to prepare a comprehensive speech on "The Power of Being
Real" that would cover a wide range of subjects in twelve
minutes—exactly twelve minutes, no more, no less. TED is
very specific about the way their speakers present. To that
end, there are also no notes allowed. I happen to be very
comfortable speaking onstage and actually prefer doing it
without notes. But the scary thing about doing a TED speech
is, there's no room for error. Your allotted time is so specific
and finite. Forget to touch upon something and you're out
of luck. Go on too long in one area, and you force yourself
to skip another altogether. This is the kind of speech you
practice in front of a mirror or a friend. Thankfully, mine
turned out really well and I was happy that I was able to do
it successfully.

So you might say that I'm a natural, right? If I didn't know me, I would. Well, you would be incredibly wrong.

Let me take you back to third grade. I was sitting in Mrs. Glass's reading class and it was my turn to read aloud. I can totally remember the sound of Mrs. Glass's abrupt voice saying, "Aliza, please read the next paragraph." As I sat there silently, I started fidgeting with a colored wooden-bead bracelet I was wearing. As Mrs. Glass called "Aliza!" over and over again, I started to tense up and tug harder and harder on the bracelet. The last tug sent the beads tumbling to the floor far and wide, rattling across the classroom. Mrs. Glass was irate and started yelling at me because I ignored her directions, was "playing" with jewelry in class and was disruptive. What she and I both didn't realize at that moment was that I couldn't get the words OUT.

I remember coming home that day and crying to my mother about the whole situation. While I was telling her the story, she seemed to already know the ending. A mother always knows. Apparently (and this was news to me) I had a stuttering problem. I would restrict my breath, and the words would just get stuck in my throat; when I tried to force them, they would come out as a stutter.

Vowels were the worst offenders. Naturally since my name started with a vowel, nothing made me more anxious than when the teacher would go around the room and ask everyone to introduce themselves. It was always the same scenario. As each child said his or her name, I would get more and more nervous as my turn grew closer. Everyone was able to simply say their names: Heather, Adam, Lisa, David. Easy, breezy, perfect. And then there was me. I couldn't just say Aliza, because I knew what would happen if I did. So I would have to say "My name is Aliza." But even if I got that out, I was lucky. A traumatic experience any way you sliced it.

It was even worse for book reports and presentations. At one point it got so bad that I begged my parents to write me a note so that the teachers would excuse me from having to present.

I guess Mrs. Glass's reading debacle was the straw that broke the camel's back. It was time to do something, my mother decided. Shortly thereafter, I started going to a speech pathologist once a week in Manhattan. My mother would drive me from Long Island to East 57th Street, where Dr. Haskell's office was located. Dr. Haskell was a wonderful therapist who taught me a technique called "airflow" that helped me get the words out with confidence. A lot of the exercises I did with Dr. Haskell were "in the field": He would take me to the corner bagel store and have me order for him. He would have me make prank phone calls so that I had to get on the phone and ask to speak to PersonX. I was asked to do basically anything that would put my speech on the spot. This went on for years. I ultimately graduated from Dr. Haskell and moved on to Dr. Donna Cooperman on the North Shore of Long Island. She continued where Dr. Haskell had left off, and by the time I was in high school—yes, I did this straight through until high school—I had made huge strides. Never, though, would I imagine that one day I'd be giving a speech to hundreds of people that would be viewed by thousands online.

I can't give all the credit to my doctors, though. A lot goes to my parents, who recognized the problem and invested in dealing with it. More importantly, they instilled confidence in me from an early age. In truth, sometimes their confidence in me had to have been false, but isn't that what "fake it till you make it" is all about? They never made me feel like I had a problem, and they certainly never made me feel lesser for it.

That's why you can never box yourself in. Labels are the enemy. You can't think, "Oh, I can't do that because of x, y and z reasons." You need to think, "I can do that *despite* x, y and z reasons." I was ultimately able to stand up and speak in front of a class because my parents and therapists pushed me to believe I could. I self-fulfilled the prophecy. If I can nail public speaking after not being able to say my name, then anyone can do anything—except lose those last five pounds, because those are impossible.

MUST DO: LEARN HOW TO SPEAK PUBLICLY

You've heard this before: Just get up there and pretend everyone in the audience is naked, right? I've never understood that. How can you pretend everyone is naked when everyone there is blatantly in front of you, wearing clothes?! It doesn't work. Here are some key public-speaking tips that I've found do work, whether you're speaking in front of ten people or three hundred:

1. Know thy content. Identify not only what you're going to say, but what takeaways you want the audience to walk away with. Writing down the takeaways will help you understand the point of your speech. Bottom line: It's important not just to speak; you need to speak with a defined purpose. You need to know where you are going and how you are going to get there.

2. If you're showing a presentation deck, don't fill it with a lot of words. People will start reading and not listening! I

always use each page to simply prompt me on a particular subject. You just need a key phrase to remember what story you're going to tell. You could also use the "lesson learned" as each title page, which makes it easy for the audience to understand what they're supposed to learn before they hear it. If you want to wait until the end to disclose your lesson, then add it into the "presenter's view" section of your deck so you know the punch line (privately) and leave the title slide as your "conversation starter."

3. Practice, practice, practice—on camera! You need to know how you sound and look when you give a talk. I hate watching myself on camera, but it's a necessary evil, so bite the bullet and do it. Are you unknowingly using helping words like "um" or "like" or phrases like "Do you know what I mean?"? These "helping" words may make you feel more comfortable, but they sound awful to the listener. Do you fidget with your hair or shift your body from side to side? Take notes on every awkward thing you do. You have to be really critical to improve. Do that until you get a result you can live with.

4. Must do: Learn to read a crowd—and tell a joke. Are people on their iPhones instead of paying attention? Did you expect them to laugh when they didn't? The best way to deal with such awkward moments is to clear the air with a moment of levity. Sometimes when I'm speaking to a room full of people and they don't laugh when I expect them to, I say something like, "Wow, tough crowd" (with a big smile), which inevitably makes them laugh. During my TEDx talk, I showed a video and when it was done, I expected the crowd to clap and they didn't—so I offered with a chuckle, "Go ahead, it's OK to clap." You see, the thing is, most of the time, it's not that your delivery is poor, it's that the crowd

doesn't know how to react. Most of the time the room will be full of strangers, and no one wants to be the only one laughing or clapping, so it's safer to just do nothing. By calling out what the crowd should have done, you make it easy and comfortable for them to do what you want them to.

5. Establish your style: Before I give a talk, I always like to share with the audience what I'm going to do (except for my TEDx talk, which I had no choice but to speak right through). For example, I will tell them that I want it to be interactive, so I encourage them to ask questions or comment throughout. By setting the stage for interruptions, when I need to take a moment to regroup my thoughts after a segment, I can always throw out, "Does anyone have any questions?" which will buy me a moment to prepare my next thoughts.

6. Edit the speech to the time needed: It's always great to ask how much time you have to talk. It makes a big difference. Not every speech can be delivered in a short amount of time. When you know you're pressed for time, you need to boil down your sound bites to fit the designated amount of time. I learned this the hard way when I went on a morning show with a well-known actor. It was me "the publicist" versus him the seasoned "actor," and I knew that I probably would get ten seconds to deliver my message, while he got the bulk of the segment. I cut my message into a short sentence or two so this way, if that was all I had, at least I knew that I would get in everything I needed to.

7. Keep your head up!! Even if you use notes—it's imperative to continuously make eye contact with the audience. I've seen too many people read from their notes, never lifting their head. That's poor form and truly shows how uncomfortable you are speaking.

8. Breathe! Remembering to breathe when delivering a speech is not only really important, it's really helpful. Breathing helps the words flow gently and easily. You will feel more relaxed if you concentrate on breathing, especially before you take the stage.
9. Smile! Smiling while speaking is something I have had to learn. Smiling makes the audience more comfortable and also makes you look better!

The next time you're watching someone present something either in a meeting or at a larger presentation, think about everything you just read. You will be amazed by how many high-level executives have no idea how to speak publicly. Some just don't project well, while others have nervous habits. Learning how to present like a pro is one of the most important skills you can ever hone in your professional life. Seriously, if you do nothing else, nail this skill! But just like with any other skill, only practice makes perfect.

I know what you're thinking: "I don't need this because I am never going to speak in front of a large audience." Well, if you ever want to be really successful, you have to learn how to do this. Public speaking starts in the conference room and can expand exponentially from there. Most people don't speak well in front of a group; it's daunting and people would rather go hide in a corner than have to do it. I get it. I used to be that person. But, if you can overcome your fear like I did, it will open another world for you. **INSIDER TIP: Good speakers not only command attention, but also respect.** It's a skill worth honing at any level and the earlier you start, the better off you'll be.

Conclusion

EVERY YEAR, *GLAMOUR* MAGAZINE HOSTS AN INSPIR-ING EVENT CALLED THE *GLAMOUR* WOMEN OF THE YEAR AWARDS. EVERY TIME I ATTEND, I FORGET TO bring tissues and boy, do I need them. There's not a dry eye in the room when these women from all walks of life are up onstage being honored. From celebrities who work on amazing causes to everyday heroes you may have never heard of, the lesson is the same: Each and every person has a voice and the power to make change happen. As we all sometimes go through life beating ourselves up over the little things that hold us back every day, that's an easy thing to forget.

In 2013, sixteen-year-old Malala Yousafzai was one of *Glamour*'s honorees. Just a short year earlier, the Taliban stormed Malala's school bus and shot her in the head in an attempt to silence her vocal support of girls' education in both her native Pakistan and abroad. Malala not only lived to tell about it, she also created the Malala Fund, which strives to empower the millions of adolescent girls in developing countries whose education is forbidden because of social, economic, legal and political factors.

When I heard Malala speak, I was moved beyond comprehension. She said, "Girls in Pakistan don't desire Xboxes or any of those other luxurious things. They just want a book and a pen." Through sheer conviction and dedication to her cause, Malala fights to directly impact girls' education and their self-empowerment. Now, at seventeen, the youngest person to ever win the Nobel Peace Prize, she so poignantly demonstrates the power of one.

Hearing Malala speak was a great reminder to me that if you have been given the luxury of education and experience, it's your obligation to share your knowledge. That's one reason I wrote this book: to pay forward what I have learned throughout my career. I hope my experiences arm you with the confidence and knowledge to power through. If you're not totally convinced that your current path is the right one, hopefully this book will inspire you to take a long, hard look at yourself and really examine what it is you want to do. After all, the journey of a career can go in many directions. What would my life have been like if I never had the courage to quit medicine and pursue my childhood love of fashion? And what would happen if you made a decision to cast yourself in a completely new leading role?

And while I didn't get this far without the amazing support of others, I never once asked anyone else to do the heavy lifting for me. I did the work; sometimes the work paid off and other times the work was for naught. Likewise, you may not get a pat on the back like you did when you brought home a good report card. Hell, your boss may not even notice all your hard work. Your career growth may not always move at the speed of your social media timeline and you may even get passed over for that promotion. But patience is a virtue and nothing is more important than dedication and perseverance. You can't quit when the going gets tough and you can't whine when the tough drags on. You are the star of your own show, but don't expect the red carpet treatment. You have to do the time and you have to pay the dues. It will all be worth it. I promise.

Every day I push myself to meet new challenges. Writing this book was my most recent challenge. I hope you continue to challenge yourself, too. Just keep pushing the limits of what you think you can handle or what you think is possible and learn something new ALL. THE. TIME. Remember that change shouldn't be comfortable, and if it is, it's not change.

So go ahead and harness your passion. Take these insider secrets with you along your journey and remember to pay them forward. Your story is just beginning and I can't wait to see where it ends...

It's time to leave your mark.

GLOSSARY: A.K.A. WORDS AUTOCORRECT SHOULD KNOW

(*S) – The homomado sarcasm symbol I invented because the world doesn't have one—and hello, it's really a necessity. *Example: I'm so glad all that work I just did on my computer got deleted. Bright side, the error report I just sent to the little man living inside the computer is totally going to solve the problem (*S).*

Anna Wintour = The British-born editor in chief of *Vogue*, a title she's held since 1988. She is considered to be the world's most famous fashion editor and a power broker who's made the careers of many.

Arthur Elgort/*Arthur Elgort's Models Manual* = Arthur Elgort is an American fashion photographer known for creating lively and relaxed ensemble images in real-world locations. His models never pose and are often in motion. He published several photography books, including *Arthur Elgort's Models Manual* in 1993, a supermodel-studded book showing life in front of the camera and behind the scenes.

Automatic email signature = Your name, company, address and contact information that's automatically appended onto every email you send.

Avatar = A picture or graphic used to represent a user's identity in social media.

Bernfeld = My maiden name, which I use in the book when discussing the early parts of my career.

Brand-perfect = An idea, concept, tagline, etc., that works within the parameters of a company or its product. Something that's brand-perfect extends the brand's story through seamless storytelling.

Call in = How a magazine requests samples from a designer for use at a photo shoot. *Example: An extraordinary amount of product needs to be "called in" for shoots. After the magazine borrows the product for a short period of time, it's then returned to its rightful home.*

Carlyne Cerf de Dudzeele = A French fashion editor credited with helping define the look of the supermodels era in the 1990s. Her quintessential high-low style pairs haute couture with everyday fashion essentials. In 1988, Carlyne styled *Vogue*'s first magazine cover under its newly appointed editor, Anna Wintour.

CelebX, EditorY, StylistZ, etc. = My way of denoting real-life celebs and other notables for privacy's sake. (Wait, did you think I was going to name-drop every celebrity I work with?) You can feel free to imagine any celebrity you want, or take your best shot and guess whom I'm referring to. But I'll never tell. *Example: Did you hear about CelebX who refused to be seated next to CelebY at the fashion show?*

Check-in = How a magazine documents that a sample has arrived from a designer. The sample will temporarily reside in the magazine's closet until it's checked out. "Check-out," therefore, is how a magazine documents its proof of a sample being returned to the designer. *Example: It's often the tedious but essential job of an assistant to check-in product, taking a Polaroid of every single accessory and writing down the date each arrived in the closet.*

Community manager = The person in charge of a brand's social media content and communications. *Example: A great community manager knows how to use brand-perfect content to create a high level of engagement with a brand's followers or clientele.*

Direct message = A message that is privately tweeted from one Twitter user to another.

Donna Karan New York = An internationally renowned American fashion brand founded and designed by Donna Karan. Debuted in fall 1985, Donna Karan New York featured a "Seven Easy Pieces" luxury system of dressing. Donna Karan herself is known for revolutionizing the way professional women dressed in the 1980s. DKNY is a secondary line that was introduced by Donna Karan in 1989. Donna Karan created the collection to address the casual and weekend needs of her and her customer. Both brands are inspired by the energy and pulse of New York City. "Donna Karan," "Donna Karan New York," "DKNY," and "DKNY PR GIRL" are registered trademarks of Gabrielle Studio, Inc., a subsidiary of Donna Karan International Inc.

Editorial = Anything you see in a magazine that isn't paid advertising. A PR person's job is to secure editorial in magazines, on websites and blogs, etc. Also known as press, editorial is free brand awareness. *Example: In this month's issue of Bazaar, they did an editorial on CelebX and her new home.*

Failed up = When a person consistently gets hired for bigger and more prestigious positions even though he sucks at his job. How a person manages to fail up is a wonder to us all.

Gossip Girl = A TV show that aired on the CW network for six seasons from 2007 to 2012. It focused on several privileged, fashion-forward adolescents living on New York's Upper East Side and was narrated by an omniscient, anonymous blogger known as Gossip Girl. I was obsessed with this show in its first season and it impacted my life in real ways. But as seasons passed, the story line went awry and I'm still angry about how it ended.

Hierarchy = You'll see I use the terms "the hierarchy" or "respect the hierarchy" often throughout this book. I'm talking about how people are ranked within a department or company based on seniority or title. In my experience, people just starting out in their careers should work on understanding and respecting the hierarchy. *Example: Using a font no bigger than size 12 when writing a cover letter for a job shows that you understand and respect the hierarchy; anything bigger and it* *would give off the impression that's too casual—or worse, that you're yelling on paper at your prospective employer.*

IRL = In real life, as opposed to just in the digital world of social media. *Example: We started off as Twitter friends but then became friends IRL.*

Last Name Syndrome = My term for when people's identities become synonymous with the company they work for. *Example: The problem with Last Name Syndrome is that once you leave the company your work for, your real name might not mean much on its own.*

Lookbook = A visual catalog of products that a brand has to offer. Unlike consumer catalogs, lookbooks are used as a reference tool within the industry, especially among designers, publicists and fashion editors. *Example: A well-designed lookbook makes it easy for magazine editors to reference a specific product, which increases the chances they'll call in that product for photo shoots.*

Manage up = To act or operate on a higher level than your job title or the job you were hired for. *Example: You get a promotion by consistently managing up, going way beyond the scope of what your job is.*

Masthead/Magazine hierarchy = A fashion magazine's editorial staff hierarchy is always listed on its masthead. It appears in every issue of the magazine and can often read as opaque and redundant to outsiders. It can also be confusing for an intern or other newbie to grasp. These titles change from magazine to magazine, but this is generally the ranking from top to bottom:

Editor in Chief
Fashion (or Style) Director
Market Director
Accessories Director
Senior Fashion Editor
Senior Market Editor
Senior Accessories Editor

Fashion Editor

Market Editor

Accessories Editor

Assistant (in fashion, market or accessories)

Intern

Mood board = A visual collage of images and text used to describe an overall feeling or illustrate a style. Designers use mood boards to develop their design concepts. A mood board often sets the tone for an entire collection. *Example: Taking words from a word cloud and assigning each of them an image on a mood board can help you easily visualize the changes that need to be made.*

Olivia Pope = The main character, created by Shonda Rhimes, on ABC's hit TV show *Scandal*. Olivia is a crisis-management expert who knows how to handle everything and everyone. She's the quintessential PR hero. Although she's not so great at love.

Pitching = Suggesting or recommending an idea to another person for consideration. Publicists pitch stories to reporters or editors. But it's not a PR-only term; any employee might also pitch an idea to her boss.

Polaroid = Refers to both a traditionally non-digital camera brand as well as the type of instant photos produced by the camera's self-developing film cartridges. Before digital everything came along, Polaroids were essential to keeping fashion closets in order, documenting samples, documenting fashion looks or model castings—basically anything and everything that happened in fashion.

PR = "What does PR stand for?" is a question I get a lot. Apparently a lot of people think it stands for Puerto Rico, but as far as the content of this book is concerned, it stands for public relations. Now you know.

Publicist = A person whose job it is to generate publicity (brand awareness) for a public figure, company or product. A publicist acts as a liaison between their client and the media, ultimately managing their client's image and shaping that brand's message for public consumption.

Pull = To borrow clothing samples. A term used by people who work in fashion as both a verb and a noun. *Examples: "I pulled dresses from DesignerX." "I need to do a pull of spring dresses for the March issue of MagazineX."*

Regina George = Regina George is the main villain of the 2004 film *Mean Girls*. She goes from being a so-called best friend to being a "best enemy."

Request = Magazines make formal requests to design houses (or PR agencies working on behalf of a designer or brand) to borrow samples, which will then be considered for a photo shoot.

Return date = The date by which a sample must be back in the designer's (or PR agency's) clutches after being borrowed by a magazine for a photo shoot (or else all hell breaks loose).

Run-throughs = The process by which magazine editors review and consider product for upcoming shoots. *Example: Dean provided accessory options to the fashion department during the run-throughs, where they'd decide which styles would ultimately go on the shoot.*

Sample = The original version or prototype of a designer item (clothing, accessories, etc.) often used as a template for the item's mass production. While the cheese samples at Whole Foods are plentiful and meant for anybody and everybody, fashion samples are often one-of-a-kind and as such highly valuable.

Shoot or shot = A photography term that means taking a picture of an item.

Still-life = A common way for magazines to photograph inanimate objects like accessories or shoes. This photography style often makes use of prop styling, key lighting, etc. *Example: Dean decided on trends and edited accessories for the magazine's still-life pages, for which the accessories would be photographed against a flat, white background.*

Text-message speak = The casual way people communicate, abbreviate or use non-words in text messages. Text-message speak should be used only with those people you're close to personally. It is not a professional way to communicate. *Example: Writing a killer cover letter means absolutely no text-message speak. Use "Dear" and "Sincerely" and, for goodness sake, no emoticons.*

The Cocktail Party Experiment = An exercise I invented to ascertain if people who converse at cocktail parties are actively listening to each other. My findings are conclusively that they are not.

"The market" = The niche category that a fashion magazine's market editor is responsible for knowing inside and out. For example, an editor's market could be American designers or jewelry. Doing their job is therefore often called "covering the market." *Example: As an assistant editor, I spent a lot of time out of the office covering the market, going on appointments and viewing collections.*

The Talented Mr. Ripley = My term for a person whose craziness is not readily obvious. As such this person fools many into thinking he is a normal, functioning employee of a company. I borrowed this term from the 1999 film and 1955 Patricia Highsmith novel of the same name.

Word cloud = A visual representation of text, where words are sized larger or smaller to denote their importance. Word clouds are often used to help analyze a chunk of text for its keywords. For example, if you are a loud person, the word "loud" in your word cloud might comparatively look like this: LOUD.

Zombie = Someone who just goes through the motions in their job rather than making themselves available to opportunities and learning all they can about the job, the company, the field, etc.

ACKNOWLEDGMENTS

Where do I even begin? I guess at the beginning is a great place to start.

When I look back on my past nearly twenty years in fashion, I honestly don't know where the time has gone, but I am certain that my career would have never been possible without the love, support, brilliance and guidance of so many.

To my family:

First to my love, David Licht, whom I met on a blind date in 1997: You are the most wonderful husband anyone could ever dream of having. Thank you for your unconditional love and support of everything I do (except shop, *wink wink*). You are not only the best partner but also the best father to our children. I know you are proud of me, but you should know that I am so much prouder of you. Nothing makes me happier than coming home to you each day, and no one makes me laugh harder than you do. I love you so, so much!

To my children, Jonathan and Sabrina, who are a constant source of pride and inspiration: There is nothing I enjoy more than hearing you laugh or watching you discover new things. The words that come out of your mouths are priceless. Your view of the world is a daily, eye-opening education for me, and in turn, it's my responsibility to teach you whatever I know. This book is the start of all the knowl-edge I hope to pass on to you. You are everything to me, and there's not a morning I wake up or a night I go to sleep when I don't thank my lucky stars for both of you. I can't wait to see where your paths in life lead. I love you more than the world and bigger than the sky.

To my parents, Madelaine and the late Dr. Michael Bern-feld: I am incredibly lucky to be your daughter. You have always taught me the importance of competing with myself and never comparing myself to others. You instilled in me the belief that obstacles were only little hills I had to climb over. I am the person I am today because of both of you.

Mom, you are the most brilliant role model a girl could ever dream of having. Thank you for always putting Ilana and me first. You have taught me to do the same for my chil-dren. I love and admire you for your values, strength and conviction. You always taught me to stand up for myself and to be self-sufficient. Your wisdom could fill a whole other book. Your love and guidance have made me the woman, wife and mother I am today. You gave me confidence long before I had any reason to have any.

Dad, there isn't a day that goes by that I don't think about you and what you would say about every little thing. Your generous spirit in helping others has been a great source of inspiration to me, and ultimately this book. I know that my passion for mentoring comes from you. I am sure that if you were here, you would be bringing piles of my book into your office for everyone to see. Thank you for showing me what it means to work hard for something and to suc-ceed at it. Nothing makes me prouder than when people say I remind them of you. You truly had the best heart. You gave everything to everyone and you have set an incredible example for me. I love and miss you so much.

To my sister, Ilana Yunis, who is one of the most amazing people I know: I am so lucky to have grown up with a lifelong best friend. As young children, we shared such a love for Barbie and, in turn, fashion—I've been in retail since the day you let me write up our fake store receipts. Thank you for allowing me to cut your hair and wash it with "Lenny" shampoo. Thank you for agreeing to let me pack you in my suitcase and wheel you around in my doll carriage. As we got older, you were always my true confidant, the one person I could share anything with. You still are. Thank you for your insight and spot-on advice. Thank you for your support in everything I have ever done. It means the world to me. I am so incredibly blessed to have you, Steven, Serena and Micah in my life. I love you all so much!

To my uncle Leo, who goes far beyond the typical role of uncle. You are truly special. Thank you for always lending an ear or a hand to help. But most of all, thank you for sharing your brilliant mind and insight throughout my life. I credit my love of words to you. My "Unci" file, filled with every blog post you have ever written about the kids, is priceless to me and I know one day, Jonathan and Sabrina will cherish reading every word. I am very fortunate to have you and Aunt Andi in my life. I love and value you both so much.

To my late grandparents, Hilda and Isaac Wind and Anna and Sigmund Bernfeld, who were all Holocaust survivors: Thank you for showing me what it truly means to be strong. Your lives have been a constant source of inspiration for me. It is because of you that I grew up already knowing how important it is to appreciate life and never sweat the small stuff.

To my sister-in-law Dr. Michele Licht: Thank you for your unwavering support, love and friendship. You, Aden and Joshua mean so much to me and I love you and the family time we spend together.

To my oldest and dearest friends: Rachel Fass Schlau, Randi Marcus Hirsch, Robyn Rahbar and Mindy Amster London, thank you for always being there for me. I cherish our friendship and all the memories we share.

The career journey:

To Donna Karan: Thank you for creating a world that I have been so blessed to be a part of for the past seventeen years. Your passion knows no bounds. I will never forget when Sabrina, at age three, sat on the floor in the design room while you were fitting a stunning beaded gown on a model. She sat there coloring as I waited for you to finish so that you could work on the show press release with me. It was totally quiet until Sabrina looked up at the model and then asked me in the cutest, most inquisitive voice, "Is she going to buy that?" We all laughed and you said, "Probably not!" I had to explain to her what a model's job was. It was priceless and it is one of the many very special moments I have had working with you.

To Patti Cohen, my longtime mentor and role model: I would not be here today without you—period, end of report. You set the standard and have taught me everything I know. From the way we finish each other's sentences to our obsessive-compulsive communication, I can't imagine where I would be without you. We have created memories to last a lifetime. Patti, you and Harvey are truly family. Thank you for everything. You have believed in me from day one and I am forever grateful. You mean the world to me.

To Mark Weber, Tisha Kalberer, Lynn Usdan and Donna Dean: Thank you for supporting my growth at Donna Karan all these years and for allowing me to pursue this special project.

My colleagues past and present are especially important to me, but I would need another book to mention them all! A special acknowledgment though to Carla Morte, Sarah Lane, Danielle Vreeland, Natasha Weber, Jacki Bouza, Jenny Lee, Adam Lilly, Vanessa Kincaid, Peter Speliopoulos, Carole Kerner, Jane Chung, Mary Wang, Anthony Conti, Felita Harris, Stephanie Reiner, Jiyup Kim, Antonio Borrelli, Kathleen Boyes, Sharon Ainsberg, Caroline Lynch, Hans Dorsinville, Stacy Striegel, Richard Sinnott, Carmen Borgonovo, Kimberly Oser, Sasha Charnin Morrison, Yamile Diaz, Jolene Eyre Postley and Vanessa Fox Halpert.

To Jenna Blackwell, thank you for lending me your story and for being such a great partner. The introduction of this book would have never been the same without it.

Thank you to Dave Kerpen and Yuli Ziv, my first friends and supporters in social media. I have learned so much from both of you.

Now on to the book:

I spent a summer in high school at Tufts University. It was there that I took a "stream of consciousness" writing course. I loved it. But it wasn't until I started tweeting that the skills I learned from that long-ago summer program came to life again. Two years later, when I started a blog, I was really able to brush off my long-form writing. The words and the storytelling came naturally to me, but I never really gave serious thought to writing professionally until I was approached one day to write a book. It's funny how roads lead you in certain directions.

It was a great pleasure to write this book. In fact, I wrote it in three months, every night from nine thirty p.m. to one a.m., once my kids were safely tucked into bed. David made me a finance-level Excel spreadsheet where I tracked my words every day so that I could stay on schedule. I love a good deadline, so it was easy for me to dedicate myself to writing every night (except on Thursdays when I HAD TO watch and live-tweet *Scandal*).

Seventy-five thousand words in three months?! Amazing, right? Yeah, not so much. When your writing style is off-the-cuff, you end up with hundreds of pages with no rhyme or reason to them. Let's just say that I will not miss editing this book! But most of all, I hope I chose the right words to put on paper in the first place. To that end, I have the following people to thank for being amazing sounding boards and advice givers.

To my editors Gretchen Young, Allyson Rudolph and the amazing team at Grand Central, thank you for believing in me and for being such ardent supporters of *Leave Your Mark*.

Thank you, Lori Krauss, Jillian Straus and Rose Maura Lorre, for your invaluable insights. Your contributions from totally different perspectives helped me more than you can ever know.

Thank you, Amanda Englander, for your vision. Without you, this book would never exist. Your dedication and passion for this project knew no bounds and I am forever grateful.

To Tina Craig, Kelly Cutrone, Erica Domesek, Nina Garcia, Stacy London and Melanie Notkin: You are all such rock star, trailblazer women and friends. I admire you all so much.

And finally, and just as importantly, to all my Twitter friends:

Thank you! Without you, there would be no book. You have broadened my world in such incredible ways. Thank you for letting me into your lives every day. We share a community in the truest sense of the word, one that I am so lucky and appreciative to be a part of.